America
And the Asian Revolutions

*Trans-***action** Books

America
And the Asian Revolutions

Edited by
ROBERT JAY LIFTON

Trans-action Books

Published and distributed by
Aldine Publishing Company

The essays in this book originally appeared
in *Trans-action* Magazine

Contents

Preface

However diverse their attitudes and interpretations may sometimes be, social scientists are now entering a period of shared realization that the United States—both at home and abroad—has entered a crucial period of transition. Indeed, the much burdened word "crisis" has now become a commonplace among black militants, Wall Street lawyers, housewives, and even professional politicians.

For the past six years, *Trans*-action magazine has dedicated itself to the task of reporting the strains and conflicts within the American system. But the magazine has done more than this. It has pioneered in social programs for changing the society, offered the kind of analysis that has permanently restructured the terms of the "dialogue" between peoples and publics, and offered the sort of prognosis that makes for real alterations in social and political policies directly affecting our lives.

The work done in the pages of *Trans*-action has crossed

disciplinary boundaries. This represents much more than simple cross-disciplinary "team efforts." It embodies rather a recognition that the social world cannot be easily carved into neat academic disciplines. That, indeed, the study of the experience of blacks in American ghettos, or the manifold uses and abuses of agencies of law enforcement, or the sorts of overseas policies that lead to the celebration of some dictatorships and the condemnation of others, can best be examined from many viewpoints and from the vantage points of many disciplines.

This series of books clearly demonstrates the superiority of starting with real world problems and searching out practical solutions, over the zealous guardianship of professional boundaries. Indeed, it is precisely this approach that has elicited enthusiastic support from leading American social scientists for this new and dynamic series of books.

The demands upon scholarship and scientific judgment are particularly stringent, for no one has been untouched by the current situation. Each essay republished in these volumes bears the imprint of the author's attempt to communicate his own experience of the crisis. Yet, despite the sense of urgency these papers exhibit, the editors feel that many have withstood the test of time, and match in durable interest the best of available social science literature. This collection of *Trans*-action articles, then, attempts to address itself to immediate issues without violating the basic insights derived from the classical literature in the various fields of social science.

The subject matter of these books concerns social changes that have aroused the long-standing needs and present-day anxieties of us all. These changes are in organizational life styles, concepts of human ability and intelligence, changing patterns of norms and morals, the relationship of social conditions to physical and biological environments, and in the status of social science with national policy making.

This has been a decade of dissident minorities, massive shifts in norms of social conduct, population explosions and urban expansions, and vast realignments between nations of the world. The social scientists involved as editors and authors of this *Trans*-action series have gone beyond observation of these critical areas, and have entered into the vital and difficult tasks of explanation and interpretation. They have defined issues in a way making solutions possible. They have provided answers as well as asked the right questions. Thus, this series should be conceived as the first collection dedicated not to the highlighting of social problems alone, but to establishing guidelines for social solutions based on the social sciences.

THE EDITORS
Trans-action

Introduction

ROBERT JAY LIFTON

America is undergoing a cram course in revolution. The experience holds a strange if fearful fascination for the country. To be sure, most of what passes for revolution is hardly that. And there is little likelihood of a political revolution in the classical sense. Those now in political, military, and police authority retain their power and remain considerably right of center. Much of the general population, in fact, remains so negatively focused upon young radicals as to give one the impression that the main effect of would-be revolutionaries is to "turn on" the antagonism of their opponents.

All the same, something in the nature of a revolutionary spirit is taking hold. That spirit is associated with a radical critique of life in America. The critique is no less experiential than political—therefore in the broadest sense, cultural—and it is beginning to permeate our entire national existence. Nor is it likely to drift lightly away. For it arises from fundamental psychological and historical forces, that is, in response to a profound sense of psycho-historical disclocation. Though America was slow in being affected by the most recent version of that spirit, there is a sense in which the last has become the first and we experience it here with peculiar intensity.

Does this spirit make America more sensitive to revolutions elsewhere? To those in East Asia, for instance? To some extent it must. The country has been rudely awakened from sleep and fantasy—awakened by guns without, and by terror and emptiness within. Hence it is no longer politically acceptable to say that America "lost China," or to deny the existence in a number of East Asian countries of powerful impulses toward revolutionary change. True, this modest ideological advance may have less to do with a revolutionary spirit than with a more general educational process permitting perceptions of international behavior a little bit more sophisticated than prior notions of good and evil. And there are moments when young critics of our society seem to retain the old paradigm while reversing the judgments—the "enemy" becomes simply good, ourselves simply evil. Such can be the impression when one hears the chant, "Ho, Ho, Ho Chi Minh! The NLF is gonna win." Yet the broader significance of the chant lies less in that reversal than in the demand that America take heed of the power and legitimacy of a Vietnamese revolutionary movement. And Americans are beginning to get the message.

We have even been holding public ceremonies to exorcise the bad old days of fundamentalist persecution of any who dared express similar insights in connection with China. I have in mind a rather dramatic panel I was asked to chair at the 1969 meetings of the Association for Asian Studies on the subject of the impact of the McCarran hearings of 1952, and the McCarthy era in general, upon Asian studies in America. More than the particular points made (which were respectable enough), what one remembers of that panel is a scene of triumphant return of men who had in various ways been victimized during that era: Edmund Clubb, the diplomat and writer, ticking off the sequence of willed American misperceptions of China; Ross Coen, author of a midly muckraking book, *The China Lobby,* telling matter-of-factly how as late as 1960 that lobby colluded with the United States Government and with the MacMillan Company to suppress publication of his book even after it had been printed; and above all, Owen Lattimore, the major academic target of the McCarran hearings, nearly breaking down as he described the "surprises" he felt during his ordeal concerning those who stood by him and those who did not, and receiving a sustained standing ovation from the large audience filling the hotel ballroom. One also recalls Howard Zinn, sometime Asian scholar and always radical critic of American society, expounding equally upon the nightmare of McCarthyism and the corrupting influence of the hotel chandeliers on discussions of hunger and oppression; Richard Kagen, the main organizer of the panel, expressing his generation's indignant condemnation of the whole McCarthy era and insisting that we continue to examine its residual poisons in our society; and finally, John K. Fairbank, father and mother of modern Chinese studies in America, both moved and moving as he thanked the group of young scholars responsible for the panel (many of whom had been his severe critics on other matters) for bringing about what he called a truly historic occasion for Asian studies in America.

Yet one should beware of overestimating the advance. Even if it is no longer respectable to speak of "losing China," America still behaves in a number of places in Asia (and throughout the world) as if those places were indeed ours to lose. And the general impulse toward such malignant possessiveness shows signs of being stronger than ever in American life. That impulse is populist in its rural, common-man, anti-cosmopolitan tones, nativist in its easy rage toward whatever is "foreign" or alien, chauvinist in its blindly "patriotic" distinction between "us" and "them." It is an impulse that not only runs deep in the American grain but in the universal grain as well. For it is associated with a broader image of restoration—an urge, often violent, to recover a past that never was, a golden age of perfect harmony during which all lived in loving simplicity and beauty, an age when backward people were backward and superior people superior.

Hence the specter of white Americans, themselves psychologically dislocated and often financially beleaguered, rallying around George Wallace and sometimes giving the impression that they seek not so much a new Joe McCarthy as a new Adolf Hitler. For this form of violent restorationism needs victims—niggers, gooks, commies, or kikes—troublemakers or friends of troublemakers who must be eliminated. (Nor should one forget mirror-image needs for "pigs," "honkies," and "imperialists.") The impulse toward restoration is a reactive one, and has undergone a quantum leap in intensity as a response to precisely the revolutionary spirit we have been discussing, as well as to the excesses accompanying some manifestations of that spirit. Young militants, black and white, themselves alternate between innovative and illuminating forms of militancy on the one hand, and a lust for generational or racial totalism and mutual victimization on the other. But it is the restorationist impulse, especially as bound up with American styles of violence, that threatens to tear our country apart, if not destroy the world.

Clearly, then, America now faces the Asian revolutions in the midst of a formidable crisis of its own. What is disconcerting for Americans to the point of despair is the discovery that *we* are a backward country—on criteria of attitudes toward race, problems of poverty and hunger, overall quality of life, and understanding of the world— and that by the same criteria *they,* the Asian revolutionaries (as epitomized by Mao and Ho) are regarded throughout much of the world, and especially among the young, as superior. But what has contributed most to our recent sense of crisis—and we see it now to be part of a disastrous vicious circle—has been our encounter with one particular Asian revolution, that in Vietnam.

The war in Vietnam has in fact served as an evil link between internal and external violence. Every statement about the war says something about America. When we tell lies about Vietnam, and act violently upon those lies, we lie, and live lies, about ourselves. Our lies about imminent military victory and about numbers of enemy dead (not to mention our grotesque preoccupation with those numbers) expose not only our fundamental misjudgement of our own power, but also our hidden technicized assumptions about all of human behavior. Similarly, our lies about the representativeness and the competence of the governments we prop up in South Vietnam reveal our disturbed relationship both to revolution and to democracy. And the self-deceptions (mixed in with but sometimes distinguishable from lies) which brought us into military conflict with this nationalist and Communist Vietnamese revolution reveal all too much about equally distorted political fantasies surrounding the ideology of anti-communism, fantasies which long organized the thought not only of chauvinists and ultra-conservatives but of "moderates" and "liberals" as well. (In saying this I do not wish to join the chorus of vilification of the "liberal," one of our most popular present-day political scapegoats, but rather to suggest that many so designating themselves have departed from the social empathy and radical dissent of the liberal tradition at its best.) These days it has become all too easy to forget (though essential to remember) that there is more to America than Vietnam.

The war in Vietnam has contributed to still another malignant polarization in American life, that of political tone. I have in mind the strange alteration between deafening rage and numbed silence, both attitudes existing throughout much of American social experience but intensified and rendered absolute by the war itself. And both are most marked in the young, as they make periodic attempts to ignore a war whose absurdity is sufficiently clear to them to render the whole subject boring—a war they feel helpless to affect, but which so preoccupies them as to exclude even greater dangers from their consideration. Thus, after reading some of my comments on the psychological and historical significance of nuclear weapons, a student told me: "I don't know. I can't feel much about nuclear weapons, but Vietnam is right here." Oddly enough, Vietnam can serve as a kind of screen for larger but more distant threats, notably those surrounding nuclear weapons. Nevertheless, Vietnam *is* right here—for the young most directly, but for all of us. And its protracted and murderous self-deceptions have rendered the American crisis both acute and chronic, both overwhelming and unending.

Most difficult for Americans to grasp, in connection with Vietnam as with China, is the special intensity with which Asian revolutionaries react to any Western presence, military, cultural or economic. If these revolutionaries are promiscuous in attaching the label of "imperialism," this promiscuity is historically understandable. It stems both from centuries of naked exploitation (which has by no means entirely disappeared), and from a more general sense of having been culturally and intellectually overwhelmed by the West. Asian social movements are, to a significant extent, revolutions against dependency, or what I would call revolutions against counterfeit nurturance. Gifts of any kind, when lacking a mutuality of giving and receiving, are likely to feel counterfeit, to serve as a reminder of weakness or inferiority. This is most notoriously true of those "gifts" bound up with a requirement that their recipients remain powerless, helpless before and eternally dependent upon alleged benefactors. We must also keep in mind that revolution in Asia is a hundred years old. Though energized and ideologically shaped by the Russian Revolution, Asian leaders have been acutely aware of their prior and culturally distinct revolutionary origins, and have been as insistent upon freeing themselves from the control of Western revolutionary movements as they have from Western capital. In sum, we have every reason to expect from these revolutionaries and their followers a strong sense of rage toward and disdain for the West—now mainly represented by America—together with a fierce quest for every form of autonomy. Nothing could violate that quest, or contribute more to that rage, than our behavior in Vietnam.

Yet there is something tentative about this dialogue of violence that we have so ill-advisedly entered into with Asian revolutionary movements. There is a sense in which everyone is waiting for something. What all seek—East Asians and Americans—are new ways, new forms and models for coping with a world equally unprecedented in its requirements for those who would transform it, those who would maintain it as it is, and those who would restore to it a mythical past. In the meantime, of course, no one stays idle. Confrontations and experiments, often desperate and sometimes deadly, go on.

Two of the most significant locales of contemporary experiment are China and the United States. The Cultural Revolution in China, with its attack upon bureaucratic structures and a search for a new mode of permanent revolution, has greater importance for the outside world than many wish to believe. But by the same token its purist totalism, self-defeating ambivalence toward technology, and nostalgic-monolithic assault upon contemporary-Protean cultural style undermine its ultimate impact even as many hunger for what it seeks to achieve. In any case China's capacity to experiment is sharply limited by the scope of her socioeconomic needs, and by the extremity of her revolutionary ideology. America imposes different kinds of limits because of its own economic and social institutions but may still be one of the freest of national experimental arenas—partly because of the continuing influence of its liberal-progressive tradition in the face of actual or potential repression, and partly because of the brevity of its history and the overall looseness of its social cement.

In America, then, everything goes on at once. Yet certain trends exist. One of these, unfortunately, involves the kind of polarizations I have mentioned, including various forms of warfare between representatives of transformation and those of restoration, with America's role in the Vietnam War infusing the entire process with violence. Yet there is also a more hopeful trend, the evolution of a humane radicalism, flexible, and open in personal and collective style, and connecting with similar tendencies throughout the world. Those embracing this humane radicalism may eventually be undermined or devoured, but if they can pursue it to its full psychological and institutional possibilities, we may reach the point where the word "revolution"—in a very new form—is justified. In any case America will continue to have catastrophic difficulties in coping with Asian revolutions until it can begin to cope with its own.

Yale University   *Robert Jay Lifton*
New Haven, Connecticut

America in Vietnam...
The Circle of Deception

ROBERT JAY LIFTON

It is becoming more and more apparent that the American presence in Vietnam is enclosed in a circle of deception. Distorted perceptions, false interpretations, and misguided actions have been continually reinforcing one another. During a recent re-visit to South Vietnam, I had a chance to talk at some length with both articulate Vietnamese and Americans, and their views revealed to me some of the psychological and historical dilemmas underlying our ever-deteriorating military and political involvement. And the Vietcong "Tet offensive" in late January and February has suddenly exposed this deception—reaching into every aspect of American activities in Vietnam—for all who are willing to see.

Beginning with the military situation itself, in official American evaluations I could not help noting an element of George Orwell's "Newspeak": "progress" means disintegration; and "victory" means stalemate or even defeat. American correspondents told me how, three or four times over the course of a year, they would accompany American troops through the same woods or highlands; each time be informed of the impressive number of Vietcong killed; and end up finding things the way they were, with nothing really settled, no new territory held, nothing secure. And when the Vietcong recently demonstrated their ability to mount effective attacks in cities and villages throughout the South, American spokesmen responded with dubious body counts and spoke of *our* great triumph. Indeed, the word "stalemate"—so repugnant to our President and our Secretary of State—if anything gives us the benefit of the doubt. It is difficult to estimate how much those Americans who promulgate this Newspeak really believe it, but any circle of deception does involve a good deal of self-deception.

Everybody seems to agree that a major cause of these military difficulties is the fact that the Vietnamese army won't fight. When you inquire why, Americans have a quick answer: "Lack of leadership." This explanation is put forth as though one were discussing a large machine in which a few key gears were missing, with the implication that if *we* (Americans) could only "instill leadership" in *them* (Vietnamese), they would then fight and all would be well. This *mechanistic fallacy* pervades much American thinking about Vietnam in general, and is a way of dismissing the fundamental human dimensions of the problem. (The National Liberation Front and the North do not seem to "lack leadership.") Americans are reluctant to look beyond the immediate "operation" into the chasm, preferring, wherever possible, to reinforce the circle of deception.

The truth is that South Vietnam is a society so dislocated and fragmented that no amount of American technology or technique, military or rehabilitative, can put it together again. The dislocation goes back at least two centuries, and can be attributed to precolonial, colonial, and postcolonial social conflicts, as well as to certain "postmodern" confusions now found in all societies. The present war accelerates processes of breakdown at every level, especially in its annihilation of village life, the main source of social stability in Vietnam. And what is too often overlooked is the extension of these disintegrative tendencies into the realm of idea systems and images. There has been a breakdown not only of social institutions but of the shared symbols necessary to ordered existence—symbols defining rhythms of life and death, group loyalties, and the nature of reality. This "desymbolization" reaches deeply into individual mental lives and undermines collective efforts of all kinds, including that of fighting a war. Whatever success Communism has had as a cohesive social force in the North or the South has resulted from its ability to provide meaningful new images and symbols, or to revitalize old ones.

While all South Vietnamese are involved in this process of desymbolization, you begin to appreciate its national consequences when you observe some of the convolutions in the lives and thoughts of the country's would-be leaders.

One formerly high-ranking diplomat I spoke to had a background of diverse intellectual and political allegiances; of long and close association with Diem; and of continuing leadership in a prominent religious sect. He spoke from experience when he described the last 30 years of Vietnamese history as "nothing but explosions." But he went on to characterize all existing political systems—"so-called American democracy," European parliamentary methods, and the various kinds of communism and socialism—as inadequate for Vietnamese needs: "We have to find our own way." Somewhat vaguely he added, "These days all ideologies are a little outmoded." I was left with the impression of a man both knowledgeable and confused, in whom the pulls of old Vietnamese and contemporary international images had resulted in a facile end-of-ideology perspective that covered over a more fundamental absence of any viable ideas at all.

Another prominent public figure, after giving a strikingly uninhibited account of pervasive government corruption (including manipulation of the then-impending elections), considered the elections nonetheless hopeful—because "people are learning to play the game of the constitution." Again, I had the sense of a postmodern distrust of all thought systems—of the whole thing being a "game" or a "scenario" (perhaps a "bag") that had to be played out but was not to be taken seriously—in a man who, like his country, could construct little that was cohesive out of damaged old goods and tarnished new ones. (He did not remain hopeful when the elections were over: He condemned them as fraudulent.)

The American response to Vietnamese dislocation and anomie is more and bigger war. And this, of course, means more deception, more claims that things are getting better and that progress is being made.

I found myself reminded of two rather terrifying psychological analogies: First, the tendency of people committed to certain beliefs to refuse to surrender them when circumstances have proven their beliefs to be wrong, but instead to embrace them with renewed intensity. The second, based upon my own work relating to death imagery, is that men are most likely to kill or wish to kill when they feel themselves symbolically dying—that is, overcome by images of stasis, meaninglessness, and separation from the larger currents of human life.

To pursue an understanding of the circle of deception, one must examine more closely the nature of the American presence in Vietnam. One is immediately confronted with the theme of the impotence of American power—of the *blind giant*. This is not to say that American men and machines count for naught, but that America-in-Vietnam, despite its vast technological and bureaucratic dimensions (one must go to Vietnam to grasp these), is incapable, *in this situation,* of doing what it says it is doing or wants to do (defend the South against Communism, help strengthen democracy, defeat the N.L.F. and the North or weaken them sufficiently to cause them to seek peace). Here the circle of deception works something like this: The giant has been called forth, fully equipped; one cannot admit that he is helpless. But the giant *is* helpless, not because he lacks strength or even intelligence, but because his vision is severely impaired. Unable to "see" the actual dimensions of the environment he finds himself in, he resorts to blind technological saturation of that environment with his destructive fire-power; unable to see the enemy, he shoots blindly at elusive figures who might just as well be his wards or allies.

Yet, in another sense, the giant seems all-powerful. There is a general feeling in South Vietnam that if America does not take care of things, nothing gets done —for there is a tendency among a dislocated people, unfamiliar with Western technology, to lean on America more and more to do everything. What is becoming clear, however, is that Vietnamese passivity is not relieved but increased by the giant's presence. This is so because of the unhealthy relationship between the Vietnamese and the Americans, a relationship marked by power on one side and dependency on the other— what I call a *situation of counterfeit nurturance*. This pattern can develop in any one-sided relationship; the weak feel special need, but resent help offered because they perceive it as a confirmation of their weakness. A classical example of such a situation is colonialism. But one also finds it in American aid to underdeveloped countries; in Negro-white relationships in the United States; and in virtually all programs of social welfare. The key problem is the denial of a sense of autonomy to the dependent party—indeed, the perpetuation of conditions that make autonomy impossible.

I constantly came upon precisely this combination of dependency and antagonism in South Vietnamese feelings toward Americans. The sense that help received was counterfeit was aggravated by the fact that the help was accompanied by a broadening of areas of destruction. Moreover, Vietnamese hold extreme images of Americans. They see them sometimes as an omnipotent force, a hidden manipulative hand behind everything, and at other times as ineffectual innocents repeatedly duped by a tough enemy. In such a situation of counterfeit nurturance, a balanced view of Americans becomes impossible; and many aspects of the American presence, as I will point out, perpetuate this imbalanced view.

The majority of Americans are new to the country and relate to it mainly on the basis of the war. For them there are another "two Vietnams"—one of fighting and killing, the other of healing and rebuilding. This "second Vietnam" is made up of physicians, agriculturalists, and providers of various forms of social and economic relief—in short, the *humane American*. But however valuable and even heroic the humane American may be, his efforts tend to be tainted by his ultimate involvement with the first group—because he is officially sponsored; or because he must depend upon the American military (dispensers of transportation and much else in South Vietnam) to sustain himself; or simply because he is American. In these and other ways, the services offered by the humane American are likely to become imbued with the suspicion of counterfeit nurturance. Their healing efforts are, in fact, associated with a strange 20th-century moral inconsistency: on the one hand, the assuming of considerable medical and social responsibility for injured and dislocated civilians (though belated and in response to outside pressure); and on the other, the willingness to sacrifice these same civilians, and indeed entire villages, to the goals of war.

There are also many examples of the *poignant American,* a man increasingly aware of the larger contradiction surrounding his energetic and often compassionate reconstructive or therapeutic work. He is an entrapped idealist—entrapped by the official bureaucracy he serves and by the mission it assigns him. He tries to cope with his situation through a form of "bureaucratic idealism," but this is likely to be flawed by some version of the mechanistic fallacy mentioned before. Thus one able young foreign-service officer working in "pacification" said to me, "If I had three or four hundred good dedicated men, I could get the job done." When I asked

whether he meant Americans or Vietnamese, his answer—"Of course, if they could be Vietnamese that
would be fine"—made it clear that he had Americans
in mind. Although well-informed about the historical
complexities responsible for the absence in such a
program of "three or four hundred good dedicated"
Vietnamese, he chose to brush these complexities aside
in favor of a characteristically American vision of the
most efficient way to "get the job done." In the fashion
of most Americans, he attributed the continuing success of the Vietcong (despite severe stresses) to their
"organization"—and sought to equal that organization
as a way of defeating it. But in Vietnam this kind of
efficiency becomes inefficiency, especially when attempted by an alien force—a blind giant—whose vast
resources can find no point of local integration, and
whose actions, even on behalf of reconstruction, are
perceived as externally imposed.

These realities were impressed upon me even more
forcefully by another poignant American doing similar
work. He was unusually well-trained (he spoke both
French and Vietnamese) and well-regarded, and he
had had extensive work in the field before assuming
his current administrative position. He outlined to me
the steps in the program he and his team sought to
carry out—establishing security, evaluating social and
economic needs, instituting necessary changes—and
then admitted that the major impediment to the whole
process was the simple fact that security was at best
tenuous because "the Vietnamese won't fight." (The
recent Vietcong offensive has demonstrated just how
great an impediment this is.) He went on to describe how he and his group would seek out a village head and coax him to participate in the pro-

gram, while instructing him on its procedures, then rush off to the provincial office to smooth the way for the village head's written application, then struggle with various forms of bureaucratic resistance (not to mention the resistance of villagers afraid of retaliation from the Vietcong). He defined his own role in all this as a "catalyst." But it was clear that under such conditions an American is less a catalyst than a *desperate energizer*—one who initiates and oversees a reaction that is not primarily Vietnamese—and, for that matter, is not really taking place.

There are many varieties of the *numbed American*— intellectually aware of death and suffering, but emotionally desensitized. Such "psychic numbing" is a useful defense in various encounters with death, but it also permits man's most extreme inhumanity to his fellow men. One of its forms is a preoccupation with "professional" concerns. Emphasized to me repeatedly was the widespread awareness among Americans of the importance of a stint in Vietnam for professional advancement—whether for journalists ("the place where the story is"), foreign-service officers, or career military men (a record of command in Vietnam, it was said, would in the future be a prerequisite for highest military appointments). And in all three groups a large number of men conducted themselves as "professionals," in the sense of knowing their work and performing well in adversity. In Vietnam, ordinary professional numbing perpetuates the circle of deception by enabling each to think only of "doing his job." Only occasionally do you encounter men who both "do their jobs" and transcend them—doctors who combine their healing with outspoken moral revulsion toward killing, journalists who, by telling the truth, lay bare the circle of deception.

I heard much of another kind of numbed American —the official who, asked about the killing of civilians, replies, "The numbers have been exaggerated, and anyhow civilians always get hurt in war"; and when asked about the jailing of intellectuals, replies, "We haven't heard about that—after all we can't keep up with everything that goes on—and, besides, we are guests in this country." This form of numbing emerges directly from the contradiction surrounding American influence in Vietnam, as well as from the deception that we are there merely to help a worthy government in its uphill fight to create a free society.

Still other forms of numbing derive from American frustration with Vietnamese passivity. Thus a U.S. Agency for International Development representative spoke of the dreadful predicament of "unofficial refugees" who camp along the roads in order to avoid the gunfire in the villages—and a minute of two later, discussing a campaign to collect blood for needed transfusions, angrily declared, "No American should give a single pint of blood to the Vietnamese until they learn to do things for themselves." G.I.s facing similar frustrations, sometimes with life or death consequences, in a strange country that seems to offer them so little and demand so much, often characterized the Vietnamese as "dirty," "cowardly," "not willing to do a damn thing for themselves," and "not worth fighting for." I heard extreme attitudes emerging from combinations of numbing and rage: "We should use every single weapon we have—including nuclear weapons. We used the atomic bomb in Hiroshima, didn't we?" Nor need one dwell on the brutalization of combatants, or on patterns of "military necessity" prominent on both sides: Americans firing at "anything that moves," and Vietcong killing those suspected of collaborating with Americans or those who simply possess needed equipment.

The psychological purpose of numbing is to ward off anxiety about death—and guilt about the dead and dying. In the case of Americans, both in Vietnam and at home, numbing prevents awareness of what is happening to combatants and noncombatants on all sides, but is easier to call forth with regard to an alien non-white people than to our own dead.

The closest to the *quiet American* among those I encountered were, alas, the resident social scientists. One I talked with, a man with a high academic reputation who had been supervising a series of studies under government contract, exuded an unnerving enthusiasm—about the country ("a fascinating place") and about his research ("fascinating" and "rewarding"). There was an air of unreality about this scholar's exuberance in the midst of disintegration: He discussed problems of South Vietnamese and N.L.F. "attitudes," and then the measuring of responses of villagers to the presence of TV sets provided by the Americans for experimental purposes. When I originally read the Graham Greene novel, I thought its portrait of the *quiet American* in Vietnam a bit overdrawn. But now I believe I understand more about what Greene was trying to convey: the American's misplaced decency, his altruistic commitment that is at once naive and arrogant in its ideological presuppositions, and which ends in disaster. Certainly the social scientist in Vietnam has been much less destructive than many of his fellow countrymen, but he has a special relationship to one part of the circle of deception implicit in Greene's concept—the fiction that a mixture of expert technical knowledge and dedicated anti-Communism will enable Americans to show the way toward a "solution" of the Vietnamese problem.

Finally, there was the *tired American,* emotionally drained by weeks, months, years in a deteriorating situation and by all the time having to explain, to others and to himself, its rosy possibilities. One should never underestimate the psychological work a person must do to maintain an illusion against continually impinging reality. One high-ranking official spokesman responded to my expression of doubt about our position in Vietnam with skillful openmindedness: "One *should* have doubts. Nothing is clear-cut." But his distorted version of events quickly emerged: "We have always been in favor of negotiations, but no one answers the phone." And he buttressed his interpretations with a series of "scholarly" half-truths, including an ingenious justification of the American presence: He referred to a discovery, by an American psychologist, that the Vietnamese "have a strong need for a father-figure" —a vulgarism impressive in its psychological, historical, and moral reach.

Even more revealing was his consistent technique of affirmation by negation. On the suffering of Vietnamese with fixed salaries because of spiraling prices caused by American spending: "There has been no *runaway* inflation." On the poor performance of Vietnamese troops and their tendency to desert: "There has been no defection of whole *battalions.*" On the burgeoning resentment of Americans: "There have been no all-out anti-American *riots.*" Here the circle of deception operated on the assumption that, since one could imagine (anticipate?) far worse developments, things must be quite good now. On the use of American influence to curb flagrant violations of election procedures, he wavered between decorous restraint— "It's their country"—and a sly admission that "We do, of course, talk to people." The fatigue and despair in his voice became all the more understandable when I learned that he had been among the minority of top-ranking Americans in Saigon who favored stronger support of civilian government. Now he was daily defending the course he opposed. For there are doves and hawks of sorts among resident American officials —and, as one knowledgeable journalist put it to me, "Everyone but the generals wants out." But the tired American must remain, and justify being, "in."

Unknown to most Americans, there are large numbers of Vietnamese who refuse to enter the circle of deception, who are painfully aware of the consequences of a situation of counterfeit nurturance. Vietnamese political leaders, professors, writers, and editors conveyed to me various messages of deep dissatisfaction.

One prevailing message was: *You are curing us to death.* A prominent political candidate, who is also a physician and given to medical metaphors, referred to America as an "iron lung" being used to help "the patient" (Vietnam) to "breathe." Then he added, with considerable emotion, "But this iron lung should be for the purpose of the patient learning how to breathe by himself and becoming healthier—not to take over his breathing for him." Using a similar metaphor, a newspaper editor wrote, "The injection of a right dose—in the right place—will cure, but an overdose—injected in the wrong place—will kill." He went on: "A moderate drink . . . once in a while will improve health and morale. But too many drinks too often will poison the blood, and eventually destroy the brain and the liver. Barrels of it will drown the drinker." Here the message is: *Your "help" is poisoning (drowning) us.*

The newspaper editor elaborated that "excessive and prolonged aid" would aggravate an already harmful tendency in South Vietnam for the city to be alienated from the countryside, and make them both "dependent on the donor country" in the way that would "sap . . . physical as well as moral strength, and render [South Vietnam] powerless in the face of a threat to its social body from the inside. . . . [This would be one of] the worst gifts ever made to this country, for it would mean eventual destruction . . . of its capacity to think, plan and execute, and its will to work and struggle—that is, to live." Here we encounter what is perceived as the worst form of counterfeit nurturance: Help meant to be life-giving becomes deadly; in political terms, assistance meant to thwart Communism speeds its victory.

In his talk with me, the editor also lashed out at what he saw as the hypocritical nature of the American effort: "We know you are not fighting for Vietnam but against China. If you want to fight China, why not go there, to her borders, and fight?" As a Southerner, he was especially bitter about the destruction of the country ("Everyone talks about the bombing of the North, but what about the bombing of the South?"). In his writings, he referred to the "preposterous situation" in which Americans supply the military force to impose an unpopular government upon a rural population, and "even . . . carry out psychological warfare and civic action to win the popu-

lation over to the government side." In our talk he
also brought forth what is for an Asian intellectual
the most extreme kind of condemnation, referring to
his country as "like a colony, but worse."

Essentially the same message was conveyed to me
by a university professor, in the midst of a quiet discussion over aperitifs, when he suddenly launched
into an angry denunciation of the blind giant's en-
croachments into intellectual spheres. He compared
the modest office of his university president with the
lavish suite maintained on the floor below by the resident American "adviser"; complained of American
dictation of educational policies, in ignorance of Vietnamese needs and desires; and concluded, bitterly, that
"Americans always think their ways, their ideas, their
teaching, their food, their way of life are the best."
Like the other Vietnamese quoted above, he was by
no means free of need for the Americans, but found
himself humiliated, and at times paralyzed, by the
form the American presence has taken.

Thus the message *You are curing us to death* readily
extends itself to *Give us back our country!* Such was
vividly the case with a young writer who had spent
several years at an American university and now be-
longed to a loosely-organized group of intellectuals—
highly nationalistic and vaguely socialist, with contempt for their government and respect for the N.L.F.
("We are against their terror but we understand them,
and consider many of them patriots"). He spoke to
me at length about America's takeover of South Vietnam, and conveyed all of his bitterness in one remark:
"This is not our country." Throughout our talk he
struggled with feelings of humiliation, and with the
quest for renewed individual and national pride. He

was contemptuous of those Vietnamese who had become French citizens; asserted, "I am Vietnamese and shall be Vietnamese until I die!"; and summed up his convictions about his country's situation as follows: "I don't care so much whether it is Communist, anti-Communist, nationalist, or imperialist [then, more slowly and pointedly] *as long as it is Vietnamese!*"

This young writer resented the Americans' collusion in what he regarded as fraudulent standards imposed upon Vietnamese intellectuals: "A friend of mine tried to publish an academic study of Marxism, but it was disapproved by the censor, so he wrote another book entitled *Sexual Response,* which was easily approved."

He alluded to the helplessness of the blind giant in Vietnam by suddenly asking me the question, "Can you sleep at night?" At first I thought he was raising a problem of American conscience, but he was referring to the artillery fire one hears in Saigon every evening—his point was that it was occurring on the very outskirts of the city. Yet he in no sense gave up on America. He recalled with great affection the warm and stimulating student community he had known there, in contrast with the "other America" of generals and bureaucrats he found in Vietnam. What he seemed to be asking for was a reassertion of the libertarian spirit he had associated with America in the past. He went so far as to suggest that, since "the problem is not the North but the Chinese" (a point of view many Vietnamese nationalists share), even if the North were to take over the country "it might want an American base in Vietnam." However one might question the accuracy of this assumption of joint interest in preventing Chinese incursion, it would seem to contain a lingering wish to remain allied to America in the struggle for national independence.

But to conclude that men with this kind of intellectual and emotional tie to the West can be counted upon to support Western—or American—political policies is to enter further into the circle of deception. Indeed, for almost a century Asian intellectuals have been emerging from their experience in the West as revolutionaries who combat Western domination. If one looks to Chou En-lai, Krishna Menon, or Ho Chi Minh, one suspects that much of the hostility ultimately felt toward the West has to do with precisely the kind of ambivalence I observed in this young writer. The strong initial attraction becomes viewed as an evil seduction that must be violently resisted in the name of individual and national integrity. And there are many ideological "Wests" to draw upon. The connection with the West is never entirely broken, but it is used mainly as a means of self-discovery.

Other frequent messages the Vietnamese conveyed to me about Americans were variations on *We feel that we need you but. . . .* A woman of about 30, who was the daughter of a plantation owner from the North and had lived in Paris for some time, was appalled at the generally corrupt and "Americanized" atmosphere she found upon her return to Saigon. She spoke even more bitterly about the effects of American-induced inflation upon Vietnamese civil servants and soldiers, going so far as to claim that many incidents of stealing and killing attributed to the Vietcong were actually the work of destitute members of the South Vietnamese army. Her proposed solution to these problems was a Vietnamese version of the circle of deception: a strongman running the government who would put to death a few of those indulging in graft to set examples for others; and more American soldiers "to fight the Communists." She seemed uneasy about reports of reservations on the part of Americans, and repeatedly asked me to tell her "what Americans think about the war." This kind of anxiety in the Vietnamese appeared to stem from doubts not only about American staying power, but about the validity of the demands they were making of Americans. Such uneasiness and guilt are always likely to increase resentment.

This combination of demand and resentment could take various symbolic forms. On a visit we made to a Saigon hospital, my wife distributed little dolls to children injured in the war. She had given away almost all of them when one of the parents rushed up to her, holding the head of a doll in one hand and the rest of it in the other to demonstrate that the doll had broken in half—all the while smiling with discomfort in the East Asian fashion and making it clear that she expected the broken doll to be replaced (which it was). The incident seemed to suggest several dimensions of the situation of counterfeit nurturance: the help needed and demanded is endless; the American giver will be resented for the imperfections of his gifts; and (somewhat more abstractly) Americans are expected to put severed things and people together—because they possess such great power, and because they are largely responsible for severing them in the first place.

I encountered another symbolic expression of this demand-resentment constellation in a young female dancer hospitalized at a psychiatric center in Saigon. She had lived for some time in London, and had returned to her country because of developing symptoms of mental illness. But she was convinced that "the Americans" had abducted her in London and carried her forcibly back to Saigon, and now wondered what the American psychiatrist could suggest to make her better. Again, Americans are seen as all-powerful —the ultimate source of both benevolence and suffering. The pattern is, of course, by no means unique to Vietnam: General MacArthur frequently appeared in the delusions of Japanese mental patients during the early postwar years, in this and other ways replacing the Emperor. But it is illustrative of the American-Vietnamese relationship.

The prevailing feeling one senses among Vietnamese intellectuals is that of despair and helplessness, or *immobilisme*. Similarly, the people seem in general to react neither with enthusiasm nor opposition but rather with passive resistance: general resistance to government programs; peasants' resistance to taxes; young men's (especially students') resistance to the army; and, of course, the army's resistance to fighting. The general mixture of lassitude, cynicism, and aggressive self-seeking pervading Saigon is reminiscent of accounts of the atmosphere in large cities in China just before the Communist takeover—which suggests that there is a certain style of American interplay with Asian corruption, of joint participation in the fiction that a highly unpopular and ineffectual government is a dynamic and virtuous force around which free men must rally. In truth, the most efficient and wholehearted American-Vietnamese collaboration I encountered in Saigon was a bar-whorehouse featuring beautiful Vietnamese girls and élite (mainly Embassy) American clientele—who had no complaints about Vietnamese "organization" or "leadership."

Since so many Vietnamese tend to reject the circle of deception, are there any authentic ideas and images to which they are capable of responding? I had the clear impression that there were three: images of *nation, social transformation,* and *peace.* To grasp the importance of these, one must remember that the human mind lives on images, absorbing and recreating them as a basis for all understanding and action. The problem in Vietnam is less a matter of "getting the bugs out of the machine," as the mechanistic fallacy would have it, than of evolving shared world-pictures that inspire and cohere. I would suggest that the up-palatable truth about the American presence in Vietnam is that it radically undermines each of the three significant images I have mentioned.

We have already observed the force of the *image of nation;* it has been rendered especially compelling by the very precariousness of Vietnam's historical status as a country, by old national struggles as well as by its recent dismemberment. A Vietnamese who is considered a nationalist wears a badge of honor, and much of the admiration in the South for Ho Chi Minh stems from his ability to make psychological contact with all Vietnamese through this shared image (enhanced by his creating a form of "national Communism" with considerable independence from larger Communist nations). Similarly, Vietnamese who feel threatened by the Vietcong are nonetheless willing to speak sympathetically of "nationalists" among the Vietcong.

Many Vietnamese I talked with stressed the South's need for a leader who could, like Ho, reanimate the national image—always making clear that men who have fought on the side of the French during the struggle for independence, as did most of the present military junta, would be automatically disqualified. One young political scientist with experience in government told me that the Vietnamese have been searching in the wrong places for models of leadership and economic development, and advocated someone on the order of Ayub Khan of Pakistan. Most looked to eventual reunification of their country, though differing on how this could or should be achieved. Virtually all maintained that the American presence painfully violates the image of nation, and that this violation has direct pragmatic significance: Guerillas with little military equipment can harass and outmaneuver the blind giant because he widely identified as an alien threat to their nation.

We have, of course, by now become familiar with the excesses that can surround the image of nation, with aggressive national*ism*. But this should not cause us to lose sight of the powerful integrative force exerted by a people's shared sense of geographical-racial-cultural destiny. The root of the word "nation" is the same as that of "origin" or "birth," and in our struggles to extend the concept outward from its beginnings in clan and tribe to include all of mankind, we may too readily forget that men still require it for their sense of immortalized human continuity.

Clearly, the image of nation is not something that one people can provide for another, least of all Americans for Asians. The refrain I heard from the Vietnamese was that "America must take a risk" and support leaders sufficiently independent of her to make it likely that they would question her policies. Both sides are thus presented with an excruciating paradox that the recent Vietnamese elections have by no means resolved: the American need to support opponents of American power; and the Vietnamese need to call upon American power to help them overcome it. This is part of what the editor quoted earlier meant by the "preposterous situation"—a situation that will find no solution that does not include a reassertion of Vietnamese autonomy.

The significance of the second general image, that of *social transformation,* is attested to by the recent use of the phrase "revolutionary development" for the American-South Vietnamese village-pacification program. The military regime's miserable record on all aspects of social transformation, especially the basic issue of land reform, renders this terminology sadly ironic. A leading legislator told me that when territory is retaken from the Vietcong, the landlords return right behind government soldiers. Yet a vision of major social reform remains fundamental to reversing the symbolic social death of South Vietnam.

While a number of the people I spoke to condemned the Communists for their "betrayal of the revolution," there was little doubt that *some* form of revolution has to take place. Thus the editor called for "a new army and a new civil service . . . [that] would have to be built up *in the field* [italics his] away from the capital and cities, around a nucleus of revolutionary men . . . living simply among the peasants." The idea sounds familiar; its proponent readily admits that it has much in common with the successful approach of the Vietcong. Our claim that we ourselves have favored such a transformation is very much part of the circle of deception. For while we have applied pressure upon a reluctant government in the direction of reform, our relationship to that government (as well as the nature of that government itself) makes impossible the actual accomplishment of transformation from within. A related deception is the dismissal, as irrelevant or disruptive, of those groups that have most strongly articulated the widespread desire for transformation—militant Buddhists, students, and younger intellectuals. They will surely be heard from in the future.

An even greater deception has pervaded America's underestimation of the significance of the *image of peace* for the Vietnamese. The idea that the South Vietnamese are determined to continue their military struggle should have been shattered, once and for all, by the results of the recent elections. Despite the ruling generals' questionable manipulations, they drew fewer votes than the combination of three candidates who had declared themselves for peace; and the most outspoken peace candidate surprised everyone by coming in second. From all that I heard when I was in Vietnam, I would tend to agree with the opinion expressed by journalists that the dove symbol used on the ballot by the peace candidate had much to do with his impressive showing. Anyone who has talked to Vietnamese during the past few months can readily sense something close to a groundswell of peace sentiment. What symbol could appeal more to an electorate that is largely illiterate but by no means indifferent to the sufferings of war and the attractions of peace? The image of peace includes relief from a long and terrible cycle of death anxiety and death guilt, and—whatever the qualifications put forth about the kind of peace there would be—an opportunity to reverse the increasingly intolerable pattern of disintegration.

I had an encounter with a "former peace candidate" that, I believe, illustrates some of the complicated dimensions of the peace image. This man was an economist who, though still in his 30s, had been finance minister in three cabinets—and his campaign emblem was a bomb crossed out by two diagonal lines. Since the military regime had in the recent past associated peace talk with such dangerous tendencies as "neutralism" and Communism, this kind of campaign by so prominent a person was creating quite a stir. At the time Americans were divided about him— on occasion one would hear him spoken of as "unrealistic" or "put up to it by someone," and on other occasions he would be praised for his accomplishments as finance minister and described as "one of the best minds in South Vietnam." No one was very surprised when, on the day before I went to see him, he was publicly denounced by the police as having "Communist affiliations," leaving his future as a campaigner, and indeed as a free man, in doubt.

This candidate told me that he welcomed talking to me, since he too wished to stress a psychological perspective. Then he handed me a brief essay (translated from the original French) in which he had, somewhat abstractly, discussed the Vietnamese as a people caught up first in a revolution, then in opposition to revolution, and now feeling "the desire for peace" as their "most powerful psychological motivation." He insisted that the elections should give the people a chance to express this desire, stressing the urgency of proper timing—since in the past there had never been the necessary combination of war exhaustion and political climate for peace, and in the future there might be little left of the country to salvage. He spoke of a "war mechanism"—a self-perpetuating system—with no possibility of anyone's winning, but all continuing to fight "because they don't know anything else to do." (I was later reminded of this when I read John Kenneth Galbraith's contention that "War turns reason into stereotype" and freezes participants in original error.) He felt that the mechanism could be interrupted only by installing a government committed to peace through negotiations; that such a commitment would cut down the effectiveness of the Vietcong, who thrive on war and chaos; and that it would evoke a strong general response in the Vietnamese people, which would in turn impel the N.L.F. and the North to join the South in negotiations. He thought that all this would take time, and that American troops would remain in Vietnam during protracted negotiations, but that once the general undertaking had been started it would succeed in bringing peace to the country.

One could raise various points about his program, but what struck me was his serious effort not only to rally the country around the image of peace but to evolve a workable plan to bring about peace. He told me that the government was spreading false stories about him in order to prevent him from running in the election, and when I asked him why the government was determined to do this he answered, "Because the idea of peace is extremely popular." It would seem that he was right on both counts: He was officially eliminated as a candidate a short time later, and the elections proved that peace was indeed a popular idea.

But images are not so easily eliminated as candidates. Once safely established in their campaigns, a number of other office-seekers (especially the peace candidate who did so well) actively committed themselves to negotiations and the search for peace. Even the military rulers were forced to make very uncharacteristic obeisance in the same direction. Many elements seem to be converging—the influence of the "former peace candidate," an increasing American realization that there is no feasible course other than negotiations, and strong pressure from the rest of the world. But underneath everything is the tremendous power of the image of peace and its ability ultimately to break through the circle of deception.

Ever since World War II, Vietnam has been living out the painful problems besetting the world at large. Thinking back to my first visit to Saigon 13 years ago, I recall mainly scenes of ordinarily well-intentioned men—Vietnamese, French, American—arguing passionately, sometimes intelligently, apparently endlessly, about what should be done, behaving as men do when confronted by a terrible problem that, however approached, will not go away. What I have tried to suggest here is that the problem is being confounded rather than solved by the American presence—because that presence works against Vietnam's only viable psychological and historical possibilities. Is it not time for the giant to begin to see? Can he not recognize, and then step out of, the circle of deception?

March 1968

FURTHER READING SUGGESTED BY THE AUTHOR:

The Two Viet-Nams by Bernard B. Fall (New York City: Frederick A. Praeger, Inc., 1964).

Last Reflections on a War by Bernard B. Fall (New York City: Doubleday & Co., 1967).

Vietnam: Between Two Truces by Jean Lacouture (New York City: Random House, 1966).

Vietnam War Stories

MURRAY POLNER

—*I think that any other war would have been worth my foot. But not this one.*
—*She was old, like my grandmother maybe . . . I fired once, twice. She fell dead. You know, I killed nine people as an adviser.*
—*It was exciting . . . and it was a man's job—the one job in the world where you're good or you're dead. I was good.*
—*I hope the Vietnamese never forget what we are trying to do for them.*
—*I can't sleep, I'm a murderer.*

Three months after his return to the United States from Vietnam, Stephen Williams went walking in his hometown of Newport, R. I. He was afraid, he now says; out of touch and bewildered. The first thing he noticed was the contrast between his country and town, standing whole and rich, and Vietnam. He wandered aimlessly, past the great mansions, the carpet lawns, the majestic trees, but his mind kept returning to the Vietnamese hovels, to a scene he remembered in which a young woman lay in a grass hammock giving birth, her sense of humor and her humanity still intact. These memories and this town overwhelmed him; he looked back at the mansions and turned away, vomiting.

Williams (the names of veterans have been changed) is a six-foot, blond, brown-eyed, open-faced youth who dropped out of his second year of college, enlisted, and later even toyed with the idea of making the army a career. He has come back a different man. "I saw the emptiness in the faces of the Vietnamese people. I saw our own wounded. I saw the refugees. And I came away against the idea of ever using another human being for one's self-interest."

Stephen Williams is one of the 92 veterans I have recently met and interviewed. Many of these men had enlisted, or been drafted, soon after graduating from high school. Nearly all were white. I had more than one hundred interviews with them, and I discovered that, to a man, their personalities and their outlooks had been profoundly altered by their experiences in Vietnam. In this article I shall present a typology of these men, describe the ways in which they have changed, and then speculate on how they may differ from veterans of previous American wars.

Shortly after I started these conversations, at first in my office and afterwards in the homes of the veterans, I met a field Marine awaiting medical discharge. He had stepped on a land mine near Qui Nhon and had lost his left leg below the ankle. He was only a few months past 19. And he was upset. His mother and his girl friend would not let him talk about the war, and his former parochial-school teachers persisted in thinking of him as a war hero.

He had never really equated soldiering with killing. "I joined the Marines because I wanted to go all the way with a fighting unit." But now, back home, he has started to wonder. "I've seen little kids killed. I've seen napalm strikes. You know, it hits the ground, bursts into a fireball, and bounces. Charley was once on a dike wall in a rice paddy. We had been pinned down by small-arms fire for three hours that day and had to call for an air strike. They flew over dropping napalm. It hit mid-way in the rice area but the wind carried it back toward us. Thirteen guys were caught and in an instant they were charcoal."

This young Marine had reached two conclusions. "I think any other war would've been worth my foot. But not this one. One day, somone has got to explain to me why I was there."

When I spoke with him he insisted on anonymity; he was almost out of the Marines, and was afraid of possible reprisals. The last I heard of him, he had apparently settled on a second conclusion, for he was speaking before antiwar rallies and supporting antiwar politicians.

Harold Byrdy, a psychiatrist (his name, and those of the other psychiatrists, are real), was in an excellent position to assess the effects of the war on the fighting man, because from August 1965 to July 1966 he had been attached to the First Cavalry Division in Vietnam. Dr. Byrdy thinks it too much to expect young G.I.s to understand the complexities of international politics while they are in Vietnam. To them, good and evil are represented by the availability of hot showers and cold beer. Combat soldiers are fighting for survival, and if a rare soldier ever thinks or speaks of the political goals of the war, it is generally in terms of conventional anti-Communism. Someone once told me that in his Special Forces team, not one of the 12 men ever spoke of anything but their most immediate concerns—a defensive mechanism possibly, but also a concentration of all their attention on the problem of remaining alive.

Dr. Byrdy had noticed this, too. "Our air strip was built on the site of an old French outpost. The French commandant's manor was still intact. Yet nobody talked about the French legacy, or how it had come to pass that we had become their successors." Only towards the end of their tours, or after they returned home, did many veterans become bitter—those whom Dr. Byrdy calls "the victimized," those who believed they had been misused and lied to. (Special Forces Captain William Chickering, for exmple, has commented that, at the end of his tour, the wife of a dead soldier wrote and asked him what worthwhile cause her husband had died for. At that point, he finally sensed that something was wrong.)

Another psychiatrist, Arthur Blank Jr., had served as chief hospital psychiatrist in the 93rd Evacuation Hospital at Bien Hoa, and later in the Third Field Hospital near Saigon. He remembered one wounded soldier who was brought in after the Iron Triangle offensive. "He had killed about two dozen VC when his best friend alongside was hit badly. Then a grenade landed next to him but didn't go off. He was so paralyzed with fright he couldn't function; the dying buddy reached down and threw it away. The kid as a result became psychotic, evoking a kind of guilt about the event."

After some treatment, the soldier's symptoms vanished and he went back to combat, as happy and aggressive as ever. He had never expressed any political convictions or any doubts about what he was doing. His primary concern was that his platoon buddies think well of him. And this was predictable, Dr. Blank says, for it was asking too much to expect that this boy, weaned on the goodness and the promise of America, to believe that his country was engaged in a questionable war in which tens of thousands were being killed needlessly. "If he ever reflects on what he did," Dr. Blank says, "it would only happen after he went home."

Dr. John Rosenberger never got to Vietnam, but as a psychiatrist at Fort Dix he spoke with many returnees. His view was that, as in the general population, there were three categories of soldiers. "There are quite a large number of doves, but they offer only tacit and passive opposition—if that—while they serve. My own feeling is that they don't seem to carry with them a sense of the tragic. Once they know you're sympathetic, they will chew your ears off about the war. They only want to get out when their time is up."

There were, he thought, just as many hawks, at Dix, emotionally anti-Communist and very angry at the doves. He believed that they tended to represent the army's "power élite"—white, Southern and Protestant—and that they seemed to see things in unambiguous blacks and whites. Cut off from what sociologists call the civilian primary groups, the service hawks had learned to depend upon the military life, often staking their self-respect on its values. It was no accident then that the hawks as soldiers and as veterans bitterly resented anyone who threatened their new loyalties and way of life.

Dr. Rosenberger was most intrigued, however, by the largest bloc of veterans, those he calls "the indifferent," those who are "really hurting in an emotional sense. They're apple-pie Americans, usually bored with politics, patriotic, and waiting out their separations so as to move into the middle-class dream they all share. They perceive this war as especially terrible, but their emotional follow-up is lacking." To Dr. Rosenberger, this is a "crisis of conscience" of which they are unaware. He believes that if these Vietvets were honestly to confront what they experienced, they might conclude that America is committing a ghastly crime in Vietnam.

"Many of the veterans I spoke with," Dr. Rosenberger told me, "thought that something was not quite right about the war. Nobody believed the body counts. Everyone was disgusted with South Vietnamese corruption. A few were even touched by the suffering of the people. And some tried to talk about their feelings—in guarded ways. But what they feared most of all was tarnishing the impeccability of America, which I suppose gave meaning to their sacrifices. And since they cannot bring themselves to do this, they often retreat into indifference—or else try to wipe from their memories what happened. The real tragedy of the war for them, and perhaps for all of us, is that they don't feel the *tragedy* of the war."

One occurrence in particular had upset him. A soldier had murdered a peasant in an especially brutal fashion. After speaking with the soldier, Dr. Rosenberger came away shaken. "The fellow was absolutely untouched by what he had done. He had no emotional reaction. It was this, more than anything else, that finally made me wonder what this war is doing to these men so that they cannot bring themselves to *feel.*"

I met Michael Pearson in a fifth-floor walkup tenement in Manhattan, not far from the United Nations. The halls were noisy with Puerto Rican kids playing. Pearson's apartment was bare except for an overstuffed armchair, a frayed rattan couch with two old, faded blue pillows, and a Dumont 10-inch television set. But Pearson himself was dressed in shirt, tie, and jacket, shaven and well-groomed, and very apologetic about the beer cans and overflowing ashtrays littering the room. "We had a party last night," he explained.

Pearson is 21, intense, almost humorless, and a chain smoker ever since his return home. He is one of six children of an Irish Catholic truck driver, and four years ago, when he decided to quit his Philadelphia high school to join the army, no one at home questioned his decision. Mike's father wished him well, and hoped that when Mike came back he, too, would become a truck driver and join the union. It was a good job, and Mike says that he had every intention of following his father's wishes. But it's out of the question now.

Mike has repeatedly marched with antiwar pickets, fought with cops, and spoken to student groups in this country and Canada. His theme is simple. The South Vietnamese leaders are tyrants, and the United States has emulated many of their most reprehensible tactics.

Although Mike was pleased to discover his ability to speak well in public, he found that his activities did not sit well with his family. His elder brothers had been in the army, as had his father, and at first they considered him a pinko. His father would not speak to him; one brother threatened to beat him up if he showed up in the old neighborhood. Only his mother took his side. She sent him a letter that he still carries in his wallet. "I respect my President," she wrote, "but I love my son, too." Of late, his father and brothers have persuaded themselves that Mike is mentally ill, and they are trying, through his mother, to have him treated by a V.A. psychiatrist.

All this troubles Mike, but he cannot put aside his feelings about Vietnam: "It's only recently that my hands have stopped sweating when I hear a jet." And on the occasions I met with him, he kept protesting how much he wanted to return to Vietnam, but this time as a teacher and healer with a private relief organization. Then, after a lengthy period of talking, he stood up and said, "I can't sleep, I'm a murderer."

He went on: "We were outside Bac Lieu, out on an eight-man patrol along with 15 ARVNs. Our orders were to move ahead and shoot at everything suspicious. My God, how I remember that damned day! It was hot and sticky. The mosquitoes were driving me crazy. And there was this boy, about 8 or 9. He had his hand behind his back, like he was hiding something. 'Grab him,' someone screamed, 'he's got something!' I made a move for him and his hand moved again. 'Shoot!' I fired. Again and again, until my M-2 was empty. When I looked he was there, all over the ground, cut in two with his guts all around. I vomited. I wasn't told. I wasn't trained for that. It was out-and-out murder. When I told that to the base psychiatrist and the Catholic chaplain, they just pooh-poohed it: They said I was only doing my duty. My *duty*? You know, that little boy only had a three-inch penknife, and I had a carbine.

"Another time, in a village, I was serving as an adviser when a woman ran out of her hut with a rifle held high above her head. She wasn't shooting it, only carrying it high, moaning and shrieking and crying, like she was mad. She was old, like my grandmother maybe. Shrieking and crying. One of the ARVNs then began shouting, 'VC! VC!' I fired once, twice. She fell dead. You know, I killed nine people as an adviser. Nine people fighting for their country against us and our stooges. Killing came easy after that."

Mike thinks he first began to wonder about why he was in Vietnam when his friend, a Negro, was shot through the temple while on guard duty. "He had tried to start me thinking about the war, but I never wanted to." His last words were to Mike: "My God, why must I die for this?"

After that, Mike says, small things began to bother him. He began seeing connections between apparently unrelated incidents. "Take sadism and killing. I saw the tie-up between the two when I watched the way G.I.s picked on little creatures, like rats and shrews. They set out cages, sometimes as many as 75, and filled them with rodents. Then they'd mock the villagers with simulated Buddhist rituals and pour on gasoline and set the rodents afire. Everyone grinned while the rodents shrieked. For the first time, I saw the connection. It was like a rebirth. When harmless creatures have to be tortured in this way, then it's easy to move over to human beings. And that's exactly what many guys did—cursing and spitting at the Vietnamese kids, beating the men, and using the women."

He reacted so furiously that he was eventually let out of the army with a less-than-honorable discharge. He's home now, hates home-front defenders of the war, chides career soldiers as parasites "living off death and killing," and goes on speaking against the war.

Hal Edwards had never really thought about politics. He was married one month before his induction in 1965, and only when he left for Fort Dix did he feel resentment at having been chosen. His father and father-in-law were upset by his dissatisfaction: Both had been in the navy during World War II, and felt that serving was Hal's duty.

"I never talked back to them and neither did my wife," Hal says. "I thought they knew more about those things than I did. But never again!"

At first Hal seems laconic, almost diffident. Yet the more he talks, the more eloquent he becomes. For the first time in his life, he relates, he is reading books—*Catch-22,* Camus, several of Dostoevski's novels, Fanon, and the literature of the New Left. And he is now wearing a one-inch lapel button on his field jacket. It reads, "I support Vietnam Veterans Against the War," and it shows a G. I.'s unstrapped helmet perched upon a rifle embedded in the ground. The button was put out by a group of veterans in Manhattan who, since their return, have spoken and written against the war. Hal has also signed their ads, usually headed "Vietnam Veterans Speak Out," urging negotiations, and claiming that true support for their buddies in Vietnam "demands that they be brought home." Hal has never met any of the thousand or so protesting veterans, but now at least he feels he is not alone.

"Before Vietnam (and everything for me is pre-Vietnam), I was in a vacuum, caught up in a machine. Never again. I was wounded twice and saw many of my friends die. I had to ask, finally, 'For what?' "

He was a rifleman, D Company, 3rd battalion, 27th Infantry. "I remember," he says shyly, almost without feeling, "my buddy and I just sitting and talking. He was saying how much he enjoyed life and how much he wanted to go home. He had been a carpenter like his father, and was looking ahead to going into business with him. And then suddenly, like it always seemed to happen in an area supposedly friendly, he was shot. When I looked down at him, his whole throat was ripped out. I think I went into shock." At that moment, he thinks, the meaning of the months of marching, fighting, and just doing nothing suddenly became clear.

"I knew we were killing the country and its people. In any other war, what I have seen might be considered war crimes. The ARVNs were the worst of all. I saw them drown people during interrogation. I saw American troopers go into villages looking for VC and hit the peasants over the head with rifles. I saw the evidence of napalm in our aid stations, where the burned included pregnant women and kids."

One minor incident sticks in his mind. "We were on patrol and someone spotted a farmer and his water buffalo. One guy said they looked suspicious but another said No, he was only a farmer. Well, they argued back and forth for a few moments and then an officer came up. 'They *look* suspicious,' he said. 'Finish them off.' Our tanks opened up and killed them both. Nobody even thought to ask first or ever worry about it later."

When Hal came home he said very little. "I would awaken in the middle of the night and stare out of the window. Several times I dressed and just walked for miles. I felt a tremendous weight on me, something that no one could understand who wasn't there." He told his wife, "I have to go this way." And so, early in 1968, he joined the pickets marching in front of a federal building in Long Island to protest against the war and the draft. He was wearing his faded field jacket, a combat infantryman's badge, his "I Support Vietnam Veterans Against the War" button, and his two Purple Hearts. A cop came up and asked if any of them had ever been in the service. "I said I had and was wounded twice." The cop said, "Too bad you weren't killed."

In *What Price Glory?*, the Maxwell Anderson play about World War I, Captain Flagg says, "There's something rotten about this profession of arms, some kind of a damned religion connected with it that you can't shake." Bob Darnell apparently shared this feeling. The day after he finished high school he enlisted. And he got a lot of emotional satisfaction, he says, out of the comaraderie and dedication he found among the men of his Marine platoon, and out of combat itself. Bob deeply believes in the cause for which he was sent to fight, and for which he would gladly return if necessary. He is a hawk.

He lives in New Jersey. His father, a World War II veteran, is a fireman; his mother, a British war bride of 1945, is an insurance broker. In high school Bob was a B student but was bored and restless. When he decided to join the Marines, he was overjoyed to receive his parents' approval—they felt it was natural that a young man should serve his nation.

Today Bob speaks proudly of the lessons he has learned from the war: patriotism, independence, and personal responsibility (virtues that he believes were first implanted in him at home). He is also proud of having been in combat.

"I was in Vietnam for ten months and only two were in combat. But if I hadn't fought, I could never again look at myself in the mirror. Luckily, I did get my chance, for this was my war. We had to stop Communism somewhere, to draw a line far from home."

Once in action, he was exhilarated. "I was now doing something for my country. It was exciting. The spirit among the platoon was great and it was a man's job—the one job in the world where you're good or you're dead. I was *good*."

In his own eyes he has been transformed into an American missionary, the carrier of technological sophistication, as well as political tutelage in the body of a superior and anti-Communist culture. He performed well in a difficult setting and saw scores of atrocities, by VC and ARVN and the North Vietnamese. He says he had also seen Americans torture prisoners, but of that he will never speak publicly or attempt to pass judgment. "I'll always refuse to say anything that can hurt my country."

His warmest memories are of the men he met. He never had any close friends at home, and in the service he was startled at how intimately the men were involved with one another. All of this meant a great deal to Bob, and it helps him talk about the five or so men he killed in battle. "I felt a real joy; in fact, I was up whenever we were shooting, especially when we were winning. The only time I was afraid was when guys around me were getting hit. But as for killing the VC or North Viets, well, it was all so impersonal. Besides, it was what I was trained for. And if you got a kill, it was a platoon status-symbol."

Still, Bob believes that he was basically motivated by a desire to change the lives of the Vietnamese for the better. Indeed, many veterans were heard saying, "I hope the Vietnamese never forget what we are trying to do for them." Don Luce, for many years the head of the International Voluntary Service in Vietnam, said he had heard that line repeatedly; several chaplains have said this was the rationalization they heard most frequently from those G.I.s troubled enough to visit them.

"I'm no killer," Bob would say, "but I do believe that the cause is just." In some instances, he went on, even napalm is necessary: "It's very effective when people are entrenched, seeping down into their caves and suffocating them." More than ever, Bob believes that questions of right and wrong, raised by critics of the war, are irrelevant: "Every time we went to napalm, the ARVN were overjoyed. I know they were. I spoke to them. They said everything would be fine if only the Reds would leave them alone. That's why I can't think of good and evil. We really *helped* those people. In the long run, we gave them something to live for."

George Ryan had enlisted. For him it was almost inevitable: He had long been troubled by a lack of close friends, and by constant anxiety. He was very short—only five feet five. He saw himself as a coward and kept looking for some way to change his life and become a hero. He fought with the 101st Airborne, and came out a sergeant. His superiors thought so highly of him that when his commanding officer was killed, they gave the platoon over to him until a replacement arrived.

George grew up in a family oblivious to his personal problems. During his high-school years in Boston, he found that he couldn't face up to anything demanding: exams, schedules, discipline, and—above all—the physical threats of his peers. He took up smoking "to look tough." (As he spoke of this, he chain-smoked, kept his eyes down, kept calling me "Sir," and clasping and unclasping his hands.) He recalled many occasions when "guys would tear me down and I was afraid to fight back. It was a curse."

So there he was, an undistinguished high-school graduate with no special interests. He ignored his father's pleas that he go to college. Instead he started shopping around for a "real fighting army" and hit upon the Israelis. When they told him that service with them might mean the loss of his American citizenship, he joined the American army —for a three-year hitch. In January 1964, he reported for basic training.

A series of events changed him forever, he says. (He said he wanted to speak of it, at least once, before time blurred the memory of it forever.) The first two events were comparatively insignificant. In Vietnam he met his cousin, an Air Force mechanic, who was there for a second time. This cousin told him that, after his return home, no one—not even members of his family—made much of his Vietnam days. Later the cousin heard, and was convinced, that antiwar protesters in California were shooting down returning vets as they arrived by plane. Both revelations alarmed George and left him deeply troubled.

Far more important to him, however, was the death of his only close friend, Walter Miller, a machine-gunner from Denver. "Walt was only 18, strong as a bull, and always laughing and happy. But one day, after a bad fight, he just went crazy, stood up, took the machine gun off its tripod, and began firing. A sniper tore off the front of his face and when I looked he was gushing blood and just making sounds. I threw up. Since then I've hated anybody with slant eyes. They killed my best friend."

George kept lighting and relighting cigarettes. Never did our eyes meet.

He had seen the senselessness of brutality, but it was remote, and George did not allow himself to brood about it. An American once kicked a wounded North Viet in the head and penetrated his skull so deeply that his own ankle had been broken. George had watched a Vietnamese suspected of being a VC thrown out of a helicopter. He had heard of the emasculation of a district chief by a VC. Yet the victims remained shadows. Then something different happened to him. He himself became an executioner.

"I was ordered to kill by my sergeant. It was supposed to be good training, but it made me sick at first." His company was near Can Tho, in a small hamlet, and a North Vietnamese had been taken prisoner. George recalls the date—February 6, 1966. "Our platoon had been pinned down for hours but finally the North Viets pulled back, leaving us this wounded guy. He had a very bad wound. Nobody wanted to doctor him or call for a dust-off [evacuation by helicopter], so my platoon sergeant said I should finish him off with my .45. I went up to where he was lying and moaning and waited for 30 minutes, hoping he'd die first. The sergeant then came up and called me chicken, so I fired.

"When I walked back to the other men, they were all proud of me. It was a big thing to kill a North Viet in battle and this, so to speak, was in battle." Does he think of it now? "Now that I mull over it, it's not how many you kill but what your friends think. My buddies said I did a good job and that made me happy. Anyway, if I had refused the order it would have meant being black-listed. I'd have been called a coward."

George says that he has never questioned what he did, nor would he refuse to do it again if necessary—although he quickly adds, "I wouldn't be happy about it." Why not? He would rather not say, but killing is fine if you've got a good cause, he tells me. Vietnam was a good cause, and he is glad to have served America. Still, he does admit that *one* incident continues to haunt him.

"It was the fourth or fifth time I had killed. The guy was five feet away when I opened up. I saw the tracers hit, the first into his back and, when he spun around, the rest of the bullets, 19 of them, into his chest." He is disturbed that he fired more than one round, and that "I never felt anything for the guy, not then or now." It worries him. "I tried to feel for him but I can't. He never meant anything to me." He remembers searching the body for papers. "He was an old guy, maybe the same age as my father, about 40."

Fred Schoenwald saw more sustained, intense fighting than any other veteran I interviewed. He was a combat medic in a reconnaissance platoon and had taken part in several of the bigger sweeps: Addleboro, Gadsden, and Junction City I and II. Before entering the army, he had worked with his father and mother in their small delicatessen, and had never given a thought to politics, or even to much outside his small town. In the half-year he has been home from Vietnam he says he never speaks of the war or the army, that "it simply never happened and I never want to hear of it again."

During our several talks he was tense, smoked incessantly, and only with apparent discomfort recalled his 12 months of combat. "I was always afraid. In fact, I can't remember not being afraid. For one thing, a combat medic doesn't know what's happening. Especially at night, everybody screaming or moaning and calling, 'Medic, medic.' I always saw myself dying, my legs blown off, my brains spattered all about, shivering in shock, and talking madly. This is what I *saw* in reality. I used to tell myself anyone wanting to send 18- and 19-year-olds to fight ought to try it on himself or his own sons. But that was crazy talk too, and I soon stopped that." He remembers overhearing a conversation that taught him a lesson. "A guy had been up to Nha-Trang, and in a bar he saw a little sign, 'If you can keep your head while others about you are losing theirs, perhaps you've misjudged the situation.' I interpreted that to mean I should mind my own business."

Confronted by what he called a "horror," Fred turned inward, devoting himself to his work. He told himself that with his medical knowledge he was serving his fellow men, American and Vietnamese. Most of all he liked helping the villagers, although the days he spent giving penicillin shots were rare. He once thought it amusing that the only Vietnamese he ever learned were such phrases as "Beat it," "Get out of here," and "Your identification card?" It indicated, he says, a contempt for the South Vietnamese, which he is ashamed of now. Once he saw a boy killed in front of his own father, "by mistake." The South Vietnamese were deathly afraid of the Americans, and everywhere he went "I saw hate in their eyes, that we should get out, leave them alone, and not give them trouble anymore."

On the other hand, George Ryan spoke passable Vietnamese, and even served briefly as a company interpreter. At the beginning he liked the people, finding them simple and generous and gentle. But after his friend was killed by the VC, and after several instances of South Vietnamese stealing, he turned bitter. "I began to think of them as gooks. They helped the VC, and had no appreciation of what we did for them."

Today both Schoenwald and Ryan feel they have been used, but for different reasons. Ryan has recently started calling his shooting of the wounded prisoner "a sort of atrocity," but won't go further. He still believes California peaceniks gunned down Vietnam veterans, and despises the antiwar critics since "they stole the victory from us." And he goes on proudly wearing his 101st Airborne pin on all his jackets, certain now that he is no longer a coward. He has, however, arrived at a definite aim. "I want to be a peace officer. I'd rather give a guy a break by arresting him than just shooting him. Maybe I've had enough, I don't know. But it was a good cause, and we should have won."

Fred Schoenwald, meanwhile, continues to blot out his experiences. "Deep down I know damn well what happened," he says, "but not *why*. I don't ever want to pursue that 'why.' I don't think I could handle it. My father lived in Germany right through World War II and served in the German army. He has never once talked with me about what he did, and I've never once asked. That's the way it is now. It never happened. It was all a bad dream. I sleep well. I only pray nothing ever happens again to make me lose that sleep. I know I couldn't handle it, not twice in a lifetime."

Many of the men I talked with were easy to classify as doves or hawks, or—like George and Fred—as "the indifferent." But many could not fit into any simple classification. Nick D'Allesandro was one.

Nick had come home from Vietnam deeply shaken. He had always been rough and cruel in his personal relations, and had thought he could "handle anything and be surprised by nothing." He grew up in a Little Italy in Utica, N. Y., where he led a bopping gang. Later he went West and joined a Hell's Angels group near Anaheim, Calif. One day he chainwhipped a truck driver, and a judge gave him a choice: the army or jail.

This young veteran now lives in a West Village tenement with Valerie, a secretary from Ohio. The first thing you see when you enter his place are two large signs. One, on the door facing the hallway, is anti-Johnson; the other, inside, denounces the war. The apartment was in total disorder: no bed, only a mattress; no dishes, only cans and utensils, beer cans and books scattered all about. Nick and Valerie drank beer as we talked. He wore no shirt; she was wearing only a black slip. Many of his sentences were prefaced, army-style, with "fuck" and "shit." But despite his obscenities and "cool" vocabulary, he was articulate, and remarkably intelligent. *The Village Voice* was lying on a desk. I mentioned to him that I had written a letter that had been published in that issue. "Shit, we used that for toilet paper." He had read the issue, but this newspaper—like all property and possessions—had lost its meaning. He wanted nothing but Valerie, everything else could go to hell.

He had wound up with two tours as a Green Beret in Vietnam, had fought in Laos and North Vietnam before the

Tonkin Gulf incident, had tortured Vietnamese men and women with electric generators applied to their genitals, and yet had emerged from the army opposed to mindless violence. He had refused a third tour and, despite his Bronze Star, almost got thrown out of the Special Forces. He had finally concluded that the war was a disease of the American spirit, and he wanted no more of it.

When he got home, he almost killed a cop who, he says, "tried to kill me first." He received only a suspended sentence because of his war record, but he thinks the cop should have been tried as well. One of his friends says that Nick, like many of the veterans who feel they have been had, is in suspended animation now, caught between his lack of values and his desire for a meaningful approach to life. At one point, Nick said he no longer cared. For the only time Valerie spoke up. "It's a lie. He cares, he really cares. Last night he dreamed he was in a village and the Chinese came down and were about to slaughter them all. He dreams like that all the time." Nick is, one supposes, trying not to forget the war but to transcend it. "People, especially middle-class types, object to my dirty language. But what possible impact can a 'fuck' have on me, a guy who has seen so much in just a few years? Anyone who accepts war and killing for any reason is more obscene than I could ever be."

After Nick was discharged he went to a Midwestern college for a semester and quit; worked six months for a book publisher and quit; and then went to work as a social worker with juvenile gangs, but quit that too—he was so contemptuous of the legality and respectability his supervisors wanted him to preach that instead he started showing the youths how to avoid the draft, and other new ways to break the law.

And so during the day Nick stays inside his tenement apartment, reading, and at night he and Valerie go out and swing. Ambition, accumulation, responsibility have lost whatever little meaning they may have once held for him, and he has become a classical anarchist.

I asked a friend, a professional Air Force pilot with 25 years' service including two tours in Vietnam, what he thought all this meant to himself and to his comrades. Gene Ferguson has three university degrees and studied at the Sorbonne and at Cambridge.

This is a different war, he believes, in that it does not follow the pattern of the past. "When I attended military-college lectures, it was always Holy Writ to stay out of Asia's mud. And we always saw ourselves as saviors or messiahs. And what did we get? Corruption in the ranks that people at home never have faced up to. This is the thing that's really hurting some of my old buddies.

"The war itself is corrupting, and I don't mean this from any esoteric political viewpoint. I mean Air Force guys can make lots of loot, extra Vietnam pay, all untaxed. Flight crews fight each other for Vietnam duty. Guys make one over-flight a month from Laos, Thailand, or a carrier and get extra pay. Loadmasters, absolutely crucial, balk at going to Germany because there's more in it for them in Asia. For those men, the rot has entered their souls.

"For others, this kind of corruption changes them in another way. If a career enlisted man doesn't come back with a commendation medal, or if an officer doesn't get a Bronze Star, then something's wrong with them. They dole it out like candy. Nothing much is required. Commanders report victories because that goes on their 'Officer Effectiveness Reports,' which promotions and appointments are based on.

"Many colonels and majors, for example, would have been kicked out long ago—'involuntarily retired' is the official euphemism—but were kept on because of the war. Promotions? Ordinarily you might wait 8 to 10 years. Now it comes more quickly. So for some it's been a ball.

"For those troubled by the war, who feel bad about the bombing, well, I've seen them try to get close to the people, work in orphanages, dole out food and money, *anything* to compensate. When they get home they don't volunteer for Vietnam any more. They put in instead for R.O.T.C., the Air Training Command, the Air National Guard, Iceland, Alaska, even Thule. At least that protects them for three years. Only the corrupted want to go back. For the medals and the money."

Seventy years ago, in 1898, this country entered a third-rate guerrilla war that lasted almost four years. Some 70,000 American soldiers fought in that war, over 4,000 were killed and almost 3,000 wounded. Today the Philippine Insurrection is almost entirely forgotten, and those American volunteers who felt impelled to save their "little brown brothers" eventually went home, resumed their lives, and were never heard of again—like all other veterans of all other wars, except, perhaps, Vietnam.

But *will* the same be true of those who fought in Vietnam? Recently, a research psychologist with the Veterans Administration speculated that if history is any guide, this crop will be no different from their fathers and grandfathers. Indeed, Dixon Wecter, a historian who specialized in the veteran's postwar adjustment, wrote in 1944 that "war colors the main stream of a citizen-soldier's life, but seldom changes its direction."

Vietnam veterans may very well follow the customary

pattern, being reabsorbed into American life passively and quietly. But now that I have been talking with a great many of them for quite some time, no longer am I certain that this group will be exactly like all those who went before.

November 1968

Hawks, Doves, and the Press

NELSON W. POLSBY

There is a bloodless battlefield in the Vietnam war which periodically gets as much attention from the President, the press, and the people as the fighting itself. On it is fought a war of words based on the public opinion polls which purportedly reveal how Americans feel about the struggle in Vietnam—how many are doves, how many are hawks, how far people will follow the President in riding up or down the escalator of war. Polls often suggest partial justification for continuation of, or change in, a policy; thus it is important to know how accurately the press reports and interprets polls since newspapers are the major source of information on foreign affairs for most citizens.

Usually we have to compare news stories in different newspapers to discern the biases, inaccuracies, and other human failings of reporters and editors as they report an event, because events are irretrievable and the news stories become, in effect, the permanent record of what took place.

But one year ago an "event" occurred on the bloodless battlefield which created the opportunity to not only compare stories in major newspapers, but to compare the articles with the happening itself.

The "event" was a poll on opinion toward the Vietnam war, which was designed and conducted by a group of social scientists in Stanford, California, in cooperation with the National Opinion Research Center of the University of Chicago. Previous knowledge of public opinion on the Vietnam issue had come primarily from reports by the commercial national opinion polls. The White House had also issued interpretations of public responses to some questions which were planted in the sample surveys of various market researchers. What was needed was a more elaborate investigation of the structure of public attitudes on Vietnam. So the Stanford group devised a questionnaire of some 30 items, pretested it on over 200 respondents in Northern California, and engaged the cooperation of the NORC for the use of its nationwide survey facilities. Money for the study was provided by more than 200 individuals in the San Francisco Bay Area plus funds from NORC.

The report was issued on March 15, 1966, from the Stanford university news service. It included a conventional press release written by a Stanford University press officer, summarizing compactly the major findings. The report itself contained a six-page essay discussing the findings in an organized way plus eight pages of tables, giving exact percentages, verbatim questions from the interview instrument, and the full cross-tabulations for all findings in the report. It also contained a two-page comparison of the results of the Stanford poll with other polls on Vietnam that had appeared in the press.

Of particular interest is the coverage by the "prestige

papers," the seven considered to be most influential with foreign policy makers. In the *Christian Science Monitor* and the *Wall Street Journal* there was no coverage of the poll. The *New York Times* gave the poll front-page coverage on March 15, and also ran an inside news analysis; later in the week the *Times* referred to the poll in an editorial. The *Baltimore Sun* gave the poll an extended news analysis. The *Washington Post* and the *Washington Evening Star* printed fairly long reports on the poll on inside pages; later—on April 7—the *Post* ran an attack on the poll by syndicated columnists Rowland Evans and Robert Novak, and later still an extended defense by the Stanford group. The then *New York Herald Tribune* did not cover the poll, but ran the Evans and Novak column and the researchers' reply.

The two Washington papers played the story "straight." They preserved the Stanford group's emphasis upon what they regarded as their most newsworthy set of findings: Although 61 percent of those polled approved of President Johnson's handling of the Vietnam conflict, majorities also approved of a number of steps to de-escalate the war. In the original report, de-escalation sentiment was indicated by many separate findings which the authors assembled into a coherent line of exposition:

■ Majorities approved four specific *de-escalation* steps:
—88 percent were willing to negotiate with the Viet Cong;
—70 percent would approve a UN negotiated truce;
—54 percent favored holding free elections in Vietnam, even if the Viet Cong might win;
—52 percent were willing to see the Viet Cong in a coalition government.
■ Four out of six corresponding *escalation* alternatives were rejected by majorities, and one alternative produced a tie.

■ All four de-escalation alternatives were favored by majorities of the President's supporters.

■ Increased domestic costs to continue the war were disapproved by majorities.

■ Large numbers of respondents who agreed to support escalation alternatives supported de-escalation alternatives as well.

Not all of these facts and figures found their way into the *Post* and *Star* stories, but some did—especially the figures on de-escalation steps. The *Washington Post* went beyond figures on de-escalation and domestic costs only to indicate that these did not agree with previously published polls by Louis Harris and George Gallup which regularly appear in the *Post*.

The *Star* continued on, however, to report a second major cluster of findings: that, contrary to published reports, opposition to the President was coming from those favoring de-escalation of the war—the Vietnam doves who nevertheless overwhelmingly approved of firm policies toward communism elsewhere in the world.

A third major cluster of findings noted briefly by the *Star* showed rejection by majorities of extreme alternatives —of policies amounting to unilateral withdrawal from Vietnam or, at the other extreme, of various alternatives involving vastly increased military involvement.

The *New York Times* front page news story bore less resemblance than the *Post* and *Star* stories to the original Stanford report. The lead sentence said that the Stanford poll showed majorities of Americans ready to negotiate to end the war. But the second sentence, in which the first actual figure was cited, was somewhat misleading. It said, "The poll also showed that, confronted with the choice of withdrawal or all-out war in Vietnam 60 percent of those questioned favored all-out war." Unlike the negotiation figures that the *Times* story alluded to but did not give, this figure of 60 percent was based on slightly less than half of the sample and was one of 16 percentage figures reported in Table 12 of the appendix to the report.

It was arrived at in the following way: The authors of the poll devised a test of the proposition that the frustrations of limited war lead Americans to prefer extreme alternatives to patiently waiting it out. They asked a hypothetical forced-choice question: "Suppose you had to choose among continuing the present situation indefinitely, fighting a major war with hundreds of thousands of casualties, or a withdrawal of American troops leading to an eventual Communist takeover. Which would you choose?" The responses rejected the "frustration hypothesis": 49 percent preferred the present situation, 23 percent the major war, and 19 percent withdrawal. When the 49 percent *who preferred the present situation* were asked to choose between the extreme alternatives, 60 percent chose the major war.

The original Stanford press release was not clear on this point—but the point was not beyond hope of clarification. The *Times* story later quoted one of the poll's authors directly, so an interview had taken place which could have clarified who the 60 percent were.

The rest of the *Times* news story neutralized the analysis offered in the Stanford report. It omitted many of the Stanford poll's findings and selected among the remainder in such a way as to suggest that for every majority backing one set of policies, there was another majority backing a set of incompatible policies.

This interpretation was made explicit in the accompanying "news analysis" by the *Times* Washington bureau chief, Tom Wicker. Wicker's analysis, headlined CONFUSION ON VIETNAM, almost exclusively used the "frustration hypothesis" question. Three times Wicker referred to this question: once to support the proposition that Americans "don't want more appeasement" because "60 percent would favor fighting a major war . . ."; once to show that "the Administration's stated objective—defending South Vietnam from a Communist takeover—was overwhelmingly supported, most significantly by the 60 percent who said they preferred a major war . . ."; and once to show that "there appears to be considerable unrest about the indecisive appearance of the war (because) 42 percent would favor a major war or a withdrawal. . . ."

This last percentage appeared nowhere in the Stanford report. It was arrived at simply by adding together the 23 percent whose first choice was a major war and the 19 percent who chose unilateral withdrawal rather than continuing a limited war indefinitely—an ingenious way of forming a coalition between two highly unlikely allies. Would those 19 percent who voted to get out, "being dissatisfied," vote for the major war as their *second* choice; and would the 23 percent who preferred the major war rather get out of Vietnam than prolong the fighting indefinitely? No concrete evidence to confirm or reject this interpretation was presented; but it is most implausible. Certainly few of the activists taking either extreme position in public debate on the issue give much approval to the other extreme.

Wicker's other two allusions to the "frustration hypothesis" figures also involved questionable interpretations. Wicker gave the impression that the 60 percent choosing the major war represent "overwhelming" sentiment— when, in fact, it represents a fall-back position for 60 percent of 49 percent of the sample—or, put another way, a second choice for 30 percent of the respondents. Wicker concluded:

A study of (the poll's) seeming contradictions and of its findings as a whole suggests . . . that a confused and worried public backs President Johnson but shies from casualty lists and paying the bill; it prefers a settlement to a war but it is determined to defend South Vietnam from the Communists.

In a letter to the editor of the *Times,* the report's authors offered an alternative to Wicker's "confusion" interpretation. Instead of regarding as contradictory the majorities that (1) approved of the President, (2) supported de-escalation steps, and (3) rejected unilateral withdrawal, the authors found these positions compatible with a position of reasoned moderation—especially when the rejection of most escalation alternatives, which Wicker ignored, was juxtaposed with the rejection of unilateral withdrawal. They said:

. . . attitudes favoring moderate steps in either direction but no extreme moves do not appear confused. And un-willingness to bear domestic costs . . . is by no means inconsistent with desires for a negotiated settlement or opposition to major escalation.

The "confusion" analysis had something of a vogue. T.R.B. in *The New Republic* said, "There is a ring of authenticity about [the poll] because it is so confused. As N.Y. Timesman Tom Wicker observed, 'The public seems to be more certain of what it won't do than of what it ought to do.' " Ignored in this conclusion were the ma-jorities *for* various de-escalation alternatives reported in the *Times*—and elsewhere in the same issue of *The New Republic.*

An ingenious demonstration of "confusion" was offered by *Time* magazine:

Oddly enough the Stanford Poll . . . showed that 88 percent would favor negotiations with the Viet Cong.

. . . In fact, only 29 percent of those interviewed could correctly define the Viet Cong as South Vietnamese Communists: the rest thought they were North Vietnamese (41%), Red Chinese (10%), or an arm of the 'government we are supporting' (4%), or else had no notion who the Viet Cong were (16%).

If this is confusion, then consider the plight of the poor reader of *Time,* who, on March 25, learned that to identify the Viet Cong as North Vietnamese was incorrect. On January 14, *Time* had said, "A more important issue is Hanoi's insistence that the National Liberation Front, the political arm of the Viet Cong, be seated. . . . While the Front certainly includes many non-Communists and nationalists, every reasonably well-informed source agrees it is an integral part of Hanoi's Communist apparatus. . . ." Thus, in a scant two months what formerly might have been a "well-informed" response was suddenly unacceptable. Confusion indeed!

A reanalysis of the Stanford poll in the prestige press by Philip Potter of the *Baltimore Sun* carries the same line of argument a bit further. Under the headline POLL SHOWS STRONG VIETNAM WAR SUPPORT, Potter identified as "some of the most interesting findings" two which showed opposition to unilateral withdrawal from Southeast Asia, and the "frustration hypothesis" results. The two paragraphs following were devoted to an identification of the poll's auspices, and gave particular attention to the fact that some of those who helped to finance the study were faculty members of the University of California at Berkeley, "a hotbed of anti-war demonstrations."

Ten column inches down in the story, Potter mentioned some of the Stanford poll's findings about majorities favoring de-escalation. But these findings, unlike the "interesting" findings which he reported in his lead, were not given unequivocally as facts, but as "claims":

In their own analysis . . . claimed to be a fuller exploration . . . than commercial pollsters have made to date, the
Stanford men accented . . . what they claim to be "widespread support" for de-escalation. . . . It also was said
that the new study . . . showed that adults critical of the
President are mainly "doves," not "hawks." On the other
hand the Stanford faculty men found that most Americans are not "real hawks" or "real doves." . . . Only 6
percent were put in the former category, and consistent
"doves" were found to be only double that number.

Actually, the figure was not *only* double 6 percent,
but rather 14 percent, more than twice 6 percent. The "real
hawks" were respondents who rejected *all* de-escalation alternatives and accepted most escalation alternatives. "Real
doves" rejected *all* escalation alternatives and accepted most
de-escalation alternatives. There is, of course, no inconsistency between these findings and the findings that most
of the 29 percent who disapproved of President Johnson's
handling of the Vietnam war are "doves" rather than
"hawks." Thus Potter's use of the transition phrase "on the
other hand" is puzzling.

On March 17 a *Times* editorial said:

There is little support in the country—as a recent Stanford University poll showed—for the extreme alternatives
of withdrawal or all-out war. But there is substantial
support for a policy of holding military operations at
their present level while taking new initiatives to seek
peace. The Stanford poll demonstrated that the country
is far ahead of the Administration in its willingness to
take such initiatives, even if they should entail serious
risks.

This interpretation was in sharp disagreement with the
Times' own news story and analysis, and was in almost

complete harmony with the original Stanford report. What accounts for the discrepancy? Can there have been hawk and dove factions within the *Times* itself? Only speculation is possible.

Newsmen are entitled to write stories as they see fit; and it is not easy to reconstruct the reasons why they may "see" a story in a particular context. Still, the fact that Wicker's news analysis was considerably more supportive of the Johnson administration than the *Times* editorial may have had something to do with Wicker's location in Washington. The Stanford poll's exploration of public attitudes could legitimately have been read—as it was by the *Times* editorial writer—as an indication that public opinion was ready to approve alternatives that had been rejected for the time being by the Johnson administration.

Furthermore, in the light of news stories emanating from the White House which asserted that public opinion disagreement with the President was predominantly from the hawk side of the controversy, this reading of the Stanford poll's findings was definitely news. Yet the Wicker and Potter analyses suggested counter-interpretations which played down this aspect of the poll's findings. Clearly it will not do to characterize the Washington press community as "a hotbed" of support for the administration, since many Washington newsmen, including the *Times'* own James Reston, have been critical of the administration's Vietnam policy. Yet we know that in many instances proximity does breed sympathy—and it is proper to wonder to what extent these counter-interpretations were produced for the comfort of policy makers as well as for the instruction of the newspapers' lay readers.

The amount of criticism that the Johnson administration has had to absorb on the Vietnam issue—especially from academic precincts—could not have been far from the minds of Washington correspondents as they read the initial report of the Stanford poll. Under the circumstances, it seems plausible to expect a press posture of skepticism toward this academic production—especially among those reasonably close to the Johnson administration, as Philip Potter in particular certainly had been.

On April 7, the columnists Rowland Evans and Robert Novak, whose column was syndicated to 119 newspapers—including the *Washington Post* and the *New York Herald Tribune* among the foreign policy prestige press—launched an all-out attack on the poll as a "scandalous job of rigging." They wrote:

> The Stanford poll . . . has become a prime document for the peace bloc on Capitol Hill. . . . Peace Senators use the poll as ammunition for anti-war arguments.

Invoking the opinions of unnamed "non-ideological professional pollsters" Evans and Novak said, "The Stanford group knew what answers it wanted before it asked any questions." The Stanford group was also charged with stretching its data, sweeping to a broad conclusion, and slanting questions. The number of professionals sharing this opinion would be difficult to determine from the column itself—at one point, Evans and Novak mentioned "two highly reputable private pollsters who constantly probe opinion on Vietnam for political clients"; at another point, they referred to the conclusion of "every professional pollster."

Inflammatory language aside, Evans and Novak's bill of particulars could be boiled down to the following argument: The Stanford group rigged its findings by slanting its questions. This could be shown, first, because they got results that disagreed with results other pollsters were getting, and second, because they resisted the "confusion" analysis.

The columnists made a special issue of the following Stanford poll question: "Would you approve or disapprove of the following action to end the fighting: forming a new government in which the Viet Cong took some part?" This, of course, was the least popular (52 percent approval) of four de-escalation alternatives accepted by majorities. Evans and Novak charged that the question assumed "an incredibly high level of sophistication" and that other phrasings of the same question by other pollsters received "resounding no" answers.

If by sophistication Evans and Novak meant political information, they could have noted in the report the high level of correct response (70 percent) to the identification of the Viet Cong, and that those who correctly identified the Viet Cong were about as willing to see them in a coalition as those who could not. If by sophistication Evans and Novak meant an ability to make discriminations among policy arenas, they could have noted that those favoring this de-escalation alternative generally did not favor soft policies toward Russia, China, or Cuba. If by sophistication they meant internal consistency, they could have inquired and ascertained how many persons favoring this alternative also favored other de-escalation alternatives.

Three days before the Evans and Novak attack appeared, a Louis Harris poll reported, "In no case is the desire for a peaceful settlement more decisively demonstrated than in a recent Harris survey . . ."—hardly a "resounding no" to de-escalation.

The set of findings in which respondents rejected increased domestic costs to continue fighting the war showed, according to Evans and Novak, "slanting of the questions . . . sure to get a 'no' answer." But, as the report itself said, this has not always been true; an almost identically

worded question by George Gallup about increasing income taxes "in order to build up our military strength here
and abroad" received the *approval* of a 63 percent majority
in January 1958, soon after Sputnik was launched.

The final substantive charge was that the Stanford group
had rejected the Wicker "confusion" theory—"the conclusion of every professional pollster"—and thus "gave
away its intent" by equating "snap opinions of a puzzled
public" with sophisticated political doctrines, such as had
been expounded at hearings of the Fulbright committee.
Not every professional pollster, however, in published
work, took the view that public attitudes on the Vietnam
issue were so puzzled or confused as to be entirely unin-
telligible. Louis Harris, for example, three days before the
Evans and Novak attack, attributed the following, fairly
sophisticated, line of reasoning to American public opinion:

> The reasoning of the public in support of U.N. arbitra-
> tion stems from two widely held beliefs: (1) such peace-
> making is precisely what the U.N. was set up for in the
> first place; (2) any reasonable solution for settling the
> war is better than expending more lives and money.

And Oliver Quayle, in a poll cited by Stewart Alsop, classified 81 percent of the American people into meaningful
policy positions, and left only 19 percent as "bewildered."

In a larger sense, Evans and Novak were raising in an
indirect and fragmentary way two problems of interpretation. First, there is a problem of standards of adequacy;
second, to what extent should public opinion polls govern
the policy choices of political leaders? The "confusion"
theory is tenable on the general principle that public opinion polls mean little anyway—that, in the lapidary phrase
of Lindsay Rogers, far from feeling the pulse of America,
they are listening to its baby talk. This can be developed
into a legitimate and meaningful argument. Enough is

known about public opinion generally to suggest that members of the general public have simple and unstable attitudes on complicated issues of public policy. The use of public opinion polls in order to justify the pursuit of any particular policy—which typically entails complicated calculations of risks, probabilities, resources, and demands—is therefore normally highly questionable.

Nevertheless, assertions about public opinion are made in the course of political debate. And when they are made, they can be subjected to tests to determine their accuracy and completeness. Thus, accepting the limitations of the sample survey method, there still may be valid reasons to try to make sense of public opinion polls. Furthermore, it is possible to think of standards of adequacy by which alternative interpretations of the same data can be compared. Two such standards would be fidelity to facts and inclusiveness. The confusion hypothesis suffers by the former standard because of Wicker's promiscuous use of the hypothetical forced choice on future alternatives, and by the latter standard because he ignored the data rejecting escalation alternatives. The analysis provided by the authors of the Stanford poll took many more findings into account than did any of the interpretations in the prestige press.

The second larger issue to which the Evans and Novak column is indirectly addressed concerns the extent to which findings about distributions of public attitudes should influence political leaders. In a sense, the implicit and explicit identification of the Stanford poll as a dove document implied that this report of opinions constituted a set of demands for certain policy choices. To those who disagreed with these policies, it may well have made sense to try to neutralize the poll interpretation or to discredit its findings. But no such demands were explicitly a part of the report of the Stanford poll. The most its authors were willing to say on the subject appeared in their published reply to Evans and Novak:

> So far as public opinion is concerned, it appears that a considerable leeway exists for American policy makers. . . . We do not believe that public opinion on any particular issue should necessarily determine what policy makers do.

Nevertheless, by dealing with a "hot" issue, and owing to its wide and prompt diffusion, the poll was used as a political instrument. But the fact that its results were apparently not equally useful to all parties to the ongoing political debate is not sufficient reason to impeach its scientific adequacy.

The coverage of the Stanford poll in the prestige press illustrates a number of things:

■ First, perhaps owing to the sharply hierarchical classification of news events by editors, the coverage of items of *intermediate importance* is widely divergent from newspaper to newspaper. (The prestige papers usually show great similarity in their coverage of items of major importance.)

■ Second, the tendency to regard newspapers as monoliths—a natural impulse when viewing institutions from the outside—received a salutary reproof from the schizoid coverage of the Stanford poll in the *New York Times.* It may be that, like many organizations in American society, the prestige press, in the process of bureaucratizing and impersonalizing its internal management and dividing labor among increasingly professionalized personnel, has also sown the seeds of diversity in its approach to individual stories.

■ Third, prestige press coverage of the Stanford poll made, overall, very little use of the carefully prepared report and analysis supplied by the poll's authors. Two substitutes for the report were, first, the telephone interview, in which one of the authors was asked either to assure reporters of the Stanford group's scholarly motives or to repeat in imprecise language the thoughts which had been more effectively committed to paper already in the reporter's hands; and second, the attempt to produce an original analysis of the tables. Some of these interpretations were indeed original; but they were also overhasty, careless, and amateur performances. This neglect of the authors' report on the Stanford poll cannot be attributed wholly to a craftsmanlike disinclination of reporters to rely upon press releases. Two other factors were also involved. The report contained many more findings than could be comfortably assimilated in a news story of even the most generous length. And second, because of the report's political "relevance," the interpretation of the poll's findings by the authors of the report was not acceptable to some reporters.

Far from focusing upon what public opinion forbade the President to do, the poll's impact seems to have had the opposite effect. As Richard Rovere put it in *The New Yorker*:

> [The polls] show that the majority that supports the President as a war leader would also follow him in almost any effort he might make toward negotiation, going so far as to approve, the Stanford survey reported, "forming a new government in which the Vietcong took part. . . . So far as public opinion is considered, it appears that a considerable leeway exists for American policy makers." That is the general view here. . . .

Soon after the Stanford poll was publicized, commercial surveys began to turn up confirming evidence of a large body of public opinion willing to support moves to de-escalate the conflict. But by then, as reporters noted, the

White House use of polls had diminished.

Public opinion polls, it is clear, could no longer be invoked in support of certain policy alternatives. In order to justify these alternatives, more compelling reasons of state had to be given. It is doubtful that public opinion was ever regarded as more than a very insignificant factor in the actual determination of policy. Therefore, subtracting public opinion from the rhetoric of justification in the Vietnam war must be considered an important aid to clarification of the premises upon which choices are being made.

April 1967

FURTHER READING SUGGESTED BY THE AUTHOR:

The Press and Foreign Policy by Bernard C. Cohen (Princeton, N.J.: Princeton University Press, 1963). An original and insightful discussion of the reporting of major foreign policy news by State Department reporters.

American Political Science Review, June 1967. See "Public Opinion and the War in Vietnam" by Sidney Verba, Richard A. Brody, Edwin Parker, Norman Nie, Nelson W. Polsby, Paul Ekman, and Gordon Black. An extended analysis and interpretation of the findings of the Stanford poll.

Vietnam and American Elections

RICHARD A. BRODY

In attempting to determine how the Vietnam war will affect the 1968 election, we are immediately faced with a paradox. Vietnam may have a greater impact upon this election than any other issue has had upon any other election since World War II—perhaps greater than any issue since slavery in the election of 1860. At the same time, Vietnam may affect relatively few *votes,* and thus be judged of minor significance in affecting the outcome next month.

The first proposition stems from the assumption that President Johnson could have had his party's nomination if he had wanted it. No incumbent President in this century has been denied this minimum vote of confidence—not even Herbert Hoover when, as H. Douglas Price points out, "he was the only *fully* employed man in America." I do not know when the President stopped wanting renomination—this will have to await the publication of his "million-dollar memoir." But it seems reasonably sure that the war, and the public's response to his handling of the war, entered into his decision.

Consider the state of the mass public in 1968—a fact of political life of which the President could not have been unaware. At the time of his withdrawal speech in March, public approval of the President's Vietnam policy was at an all-time low (26 percent); the President had not had majority support in the polls since April 1966; and, with the exception of May 1967, the polls had not recorded a plurality of "approvers" since December 1966.

The President has made it abundantly clear that, for him, public opinion does not make public policy. But policy-makers can be elected or defeated by the feelings behind responses to opinion surveys. And the public mood in March did not bode well for November.

Public-opinion trends are, of course, far from the complete story. If the war had been going well, the President could expect that, once the public had been informed, Vietnam could have been turned from an electoral deficit into an asset. The Tet offensive must have aborted this expectation. After Tet, it became hard to deny that the public's view of the war had more to commend it than the generals'.

The public's response to the war, America's poor showing in the war itself, and the link between war-spending and domestic unrest have already had a profound effect on the 1968 election. Not only have they contributed to a President's removing himself from the contest; they have also created centers of opposition within the incumbent's party, and they have given voters an issue on which to focus. If, in addition, we accord Vietnam a role in the crisis of the cities, we would have to say that it has given the voters their *two* most salient issues.How is it possible, then, to believe that Vietnam may affect relatively few votes in November?

Let us consider what we know about the determinants of the voting act—or the "formula" for voting behavior. In this formula we can place information about the current state of the war, the status of the Paris negotiations, and such information on public opinion as is available. Within fairly broad limits, these steps will allow us to preview the role of the Vietnam issue in the 1968 election.

The investigation of why people vote the way they do has been of interest to American scholars for a long time; analytic studies, using survey-generated data, go back to the 1940s with the pioneering efforts of the Bureau of Applied Social Research (Columbia) and the Survey Research Center (Michigan). A major conclusion of these studies can be summarized by the following relatively well-confirmed proposition: *People vote the way they do primarily because of the way they feel about the political parties—their "party identification."*

Party identification is defined by the Michigan group as "the sense of personal attachment the individual feels toward the [political] group of his choice." It is customary to classify party identifications into seven categories, running from "strong Democrat" to "strong Republican," with three groups of Independents. Table 1 gives the percentages of Americans in these categories over the past 16 years, covering eight Presidential and off-year elections.

FROM STRONG DEMOCRAT TO STRONG REPUBLICAN   (Table 1)
Distribution of Party Identifications

Party Identification

| Year | Democrat | | | Independent | | Republican | | Other |
	Strong	Weak	Dem.	Ind.	Rep.	Weak	Strong	
1952	22%	25%	10%	5%	7%	14%	13%	4%
1954	22	25	9	7	6	14	13	4
1956	21	23	7	9	8	14	15	3
1958	23	24	7	8	4	16	13	5
1960	21	25	8	8	7	13	14	4
1962	23	23	8	8	6	16	12	4
1964	26	25	9	8	6	13	11	2
1966	18	28	9	12	7	15	10	1
1968	18	22	9	17	8	13	11	2

Source: Arthur Wolfe, "Some Results of the 1966-67 Election Study" (Memorandum, Survey Research Center, University of Michigan, May 25, 1967). The 1968 data are from the Stanford/Pittsburgh Survey.

Four things are noteworthy about this table:
■ For a decade (1952-1962), the distribution of basic political loyalties among American voters was remarkably stable;
■ the Goldwater candidacy was accompanied by a significant rise in the percentage of "strong" Democrats;
■ since 1964, there has been a significant drop-off in the percentage of "strong" Democrats, not only from the 1964 high, but also from the average for 1952 through 1964; and
■ of late, there appears to be a trend towards independence and away from identification with either party.

These changes are not trivial, for—as Table 2 shows—a person's party identification is strongly related to his vote. And if the trend toward weaker party identification continues, it may signal a radical change in people's voting behavior.

Now, as noted, the percentages of "strong" Democrats, "weak" Republicans, and so on, have been rather stable in recent years. And yet election outcomes have been a mixed bag, with Democrats winning one election, Republicans the next. Therefore, while party identifications are indispensable for explaining how people vote, they are of limited usefulness in explaining any *particular election*. Sometimes, in fact, it is the switch from party identifications that decides an election. Clearly, then, additional factors must be found to help explain election results.

These other factors have been sought in six general areas:

1. The voter's attitude about the Democratic candidate as a person;
2. His attitude about the Republican candidate as

a person;

3. His attitude about the stance of the parties and candidates on helping various groups, like businessmen or Negroes;

4. His attitude about the stance of the parties and candidates on domestic policy;

5. His attitude about the stance of the parties and candidates on foreign policy; and

6. His attitude about the performance of the parties in the nation's affairs.

VOTING THE PARTY LINE (Table 2)
Relation of Party Identification
to Presidential Vote

	Party Identification				
	Democrat		Indepen-	Republican	
Year/Vote	Strong	Weak	dent*	Weak	Strong
1952					
Eisenhower	16%	38%	67%	94%	99%
Stevenson	84	62	33	6	1
1956					
Eisenhower	15	37	73	93	99
Stevenson	85	63	27	7	1
1960					
Nixon	9	29	54	87	98
Kennedy	91	71	46	13	2
1964					
Goldwater	5	18	34	57	90
Johnson	95	82	66	43	10

Source: Data gathered by the Survey Research Center, University of Michigan; made available through the Inter-University Consortium for Political Research.
* The three categories of Independents are collapsed together.

These "partisan attitudes" are by no means independent, and the extent of their interdependence complicates any analysis of people's voting decisions. Moreover, scholars disagree on the question of *causality* among these partisan attitudes. Does a voter like (say) a Democratic candidate *because* that voter approves of the candidate's views on foreign policy, or does the voter approve of the candidate's foreign-policy views and *therefore* like him as a candidate? And what of party identification—does the fact that a voter is a strong Republican cause him (say) to approve of a Republican candidate, or does that voter's approval of the Republican candidate make the voter a strong Republican? Angus Campbell and his associates maintain the former—that *party identification* causes *partisan attitude;* V.O. Key maintains the latter—that *partisan attitude* causes *party identification.* This is not a trivial question, because if his being a Democrat or Republican leads a voter to decide on the issues, we might view him as a relatively *automatic* decision-maker; if from the issues he decides whether to become a Democrat, Republican, or Independent, we might view him as a relatively *rational* decision-maker.

Besides partisan attitudes and party identification, there are still other factors that determine how a person will vote. These other factors were suggested by Arthur Goldberg:

■ the voter's social background (his father's social class);

■ the voter's socialization (his father's party identification); and

■ the voter's status (his social class).

According to Goldberg, these factors are *mediated* by the voter's partisan attitudes and party identification.

In other words, a person's vote is causally linked to his partisan attitudes plus his party identification. And his partisan attitudes and his party identification are *in turn* linked to his social background, socialization, and status. In short, social background + socialization + status → partisan attitudes + party identification → voting behavior. This formula accounts for half of the variation in the vote. Thus, it is a very powerful theory indeed—but still a fair distance from completely explaining voting behavior.

Now, these general studies of electoral decision-making are not very helpful in explaining what role foreign policy plays in determining how a person will vote. Those few studies of foreign policy's effect on the vote, moreover, are suggestive rather than conclusive.

George Belknap and Angus Campbell have studied the relationship between the way a person plans to vote (far in advance of an election) and that person's attitudes about foreign policy. In one investigation, they found that when President Truman's public image was at its worst (according to public-opinion trends), there was a strong relationship between a person's *satisfaction* with a party's foreign policy and his voting intention. That is, if a voter approved of Truman's foreign policy, that voter was likely to vote for the forthcoming Democratic candidate in 1952, whoever he might be.

According to Donald Stokes's estimate, the Republican landslide in 1952 in part reflected the voters' dissatisfaction with the Democratic administration's handling of foreign policy—*and* with its performance in general. The Republicans and General Eisenhower *netted* about 3.5 percent of the 1952 vote from foreign-policy attitudes and 5.5 percent from attitudes related to the general performance by the Democratic administration. Clearly then, foreign policy is a significant factor in determining how people will vote—or at least it was in 1952, when the Korean War was still being fought.

Unfortunately, since Belknap and Campbell did not investigate how voters felt about domestic issues, and since when they made their study the voters did not know that Stevenson and Eisenhower would be the candidates, their study does not help us assess the importance of foreign policy in relation to *other* influences on the vote (e.g., domestic issues and the candidates themselves).

Before leaving this brief summary of their 16-year-old study, one more item of interest should be noted. Belknap and Campbell constructed a four-step "dove-hawk" scale (from "get out of Korea and stay out" to "invade China"), and found remarkably equal percentages of all four scale-types, from doves to hawks, among those planning to vote Democratic, those planning to vote Republican, and among those who had not made up their minds for whom to vote.

Thus, they discovered that a person's *policy preferences* were *not* related to his voting intention. This remarkable finding—taken together with the finding that a person's satisfaction with a party's foreign policy *is* related to his voting intention—suggests (and only suggests) that *a person's vote more nearly reflects his reaction to a party's past performance on an issue rather than his desire to give a mandate for a new policy direction.*

Warren E. Miller has focused on the net percentage of the vote that the Republicans have been gaining or losing from voters' foreign-policy attitudes, and from the picture of the Democrats as the "party of war."

From 1952 to 1964, the Republicans' net gain from foreign policy declined from 3.5 percent to −0.5 percent. This shift was accompanied by an exponential rise in the percentage of those who thought the Dem-

KEEPING US OUT OF WAR
Evaluation of Parties' Capability in Keeping the U.S.
Out of War or a Bigger War (Table 3)

Problem would be handled*	1956	1960	Year 1964	1966	1968
Better by Democrats	7%	15%	38%	11%	12%
Same by both parties	45	46	46	57	55
Better by Republicans	40	29	12	15	17
Don't know	7	8	4	17	16
Not ascertained	1	2	—	—	—

Sources: Warren Miller, "Voting and Foreign Policy," in James Rosenau, ed., *Domestic Sources of Foreign Policy;* Wolfe, *op. cit.* The 1968 data are from the Stanford/Pittsburgh Survey, New York: Free Press (1967).
* The question used in these five surveys reads, "Now looking ahead, do you think the problem of keeping out of a war [1964 & 1966, 'a bigger war'] would be handled better in the next four years by the Republicans, or by the Democrats, or about the same by both?"

ocrats *better* "able to keep us out of war." And since, from 1956 to 1964, the percentage believing the two parties *equally* capable of keeping us out of war remained about 46 percent, the improved image of the Democrats was entirely at Republican expense. Table 3 documents these trends, and also shows the dramatic change that has taken place since 1964. In 1968, only 12 percent of the voters think that the Democrats are better at keeping us out of war—as compared with 38 percent in 1964, and as compared with 17 percent thinking that the Republicans are better. Yet although the Democrats have lost ground since 1964, their loss has not proved much of a gain for the Republicans.

V.O. Key, writing about the 1952 election, tells us: ". . . the conclusion is inescapable that the election marked no majority rejection of the major trends of domestic policy under the New Deal and the Fair Deal. . . . The major content of the electoral decision related to the performance of the Truman administration in the field of foreign policy." Key's data appear in Tables 4 and 5.

1956 Presidential vote in relation to voters' party identification & to opinion about party capability in handling the "problem of keeping out of war" (Table 4)

Party Identification	Better by Democrats	Same by Both	Better by Republicans
	Voting Democratic	Voting Democratic	Voting Democratic
Strong Democrat	87%	90%	47%
Weak Democrat	96	71	24
Independent	—	42	11
Weak Republican	—	14	2
Strong Republican	—	—	—

Source: V.O. Key, *Public Opinion and American Democracy*.

Table 5 also illustrates a point that Philip E. Converse states quite succinctly: ". . . the actual vote in any election, although influenced by short-term forces, is still largely determined by [the] distribution of [party loyalties]."

Table 5 offers some data for resolving this apparent disagreement between Key and Converse. The table shows that, of strong Democrats who said they did not know whether the Truman administration was responsible for the loss of China, 84 percent voted for Stevenson. Of the strong Democrats who absolved the Truman administration, 89 percent voted for Stevenson. The respective percentages for weak Democrats were 66 percent and 67 percent.

Several questions immediately suggest themselves. Why was there so little difference between those who gave Don't Know responses and those who absolved the United States? The difference between strong Democrats was 5 percent; the difference between weak Democrats was 1 percent. Does this suggest that the loss of China was less significant for them than Key would have us believe? Was America's China policy not important to those Democrats who took the drastic step of voting Republican? If so, then Converse would seem to be correct—party identification is far more important in determining the votes of Democrats and Republicans than foreign policy is.

On the other hand, the defection rate among Democrats who thought the loss of China *was* our fault was far higher than among Democrats who were unsure or Democrats who absolved the United States. Since more Democrats-who-felt-the-loss-of-China-was-our-fault seemed to vote Republican as a consequence, was the issue more important for them than for the other two groups of Democrats?

In short, it would seem that both Key and Converse are partly right. Among Democrats and Republicans, foreign policy can determine votes—but mainly among those people whose own views are decidedly antagonistic to the party that they traditionally support. (Among Independents, of course, foreign policy can be decisive all across the board.)

Now let me try to relate all of this research to the 1968 election.

In the first place, what was true in 1952—that those Democrats who felt the United States was responsible for the loss of China were more likely to defect than other Democrats—was also true in 1956, but on another important aspect of foreign-policy performance. As Table 4 shows, in 1956 those Democrats who thought that the Republicans were "better able to keep us out of war" defected at a much higher rate than other Democrats. In both of these elections, of course, the Democrats lost.

We have only presumptive evidence on the role of foreign policy in the elections of 1960 and 1964. But the declining net percentage of the vote that the Republicans gained from voters' foreign-policy attitudes, and the Republicans' declining image as the "party of peace," offers fertile grounds for speculation about their defeats. We could also speculate about the possible impact on the 1968 election of the 26 percent drop, from 1964, in those voters who think the Democrats "better able to keep us out of a bigger war."

1952 Presidential vote in relation to voters' party identification & their opinion on U.S. responsibility for Communist capture of China   (Table 5)

Party Identification	Opinion on China Policy*		
	Our Fault	Don't Know	Nothing U.S. Could Do
	Voting Democratic	Voting Democratic	Voting Democratic
Strong Democrat	69%	84%	89%
Weak Democrat	40	66	67
Independent	28	20	45
Weak Republican	3	6	8
Strong Republican	1	0	0

Source: V.O. Key, *op. cit.*
* Opinion on China policy is represented by responses to the question, "Some people feel that it was our government's fault that China went Communist, others say there was nothing we could do stop it. How do you feel about this?"

But I really should not apologize for offering parallels between 1952 and the upcoming election. The foreign-policy issues in the more recent 1956, 1960, and 1964 elections were of less importance to the voters, so these elections were less like 1968 than 1952 was. (This may be surprising about 1964, but according to Stokes's data foreign policy was then one-fourth as important as domestic policy.) The fact that the 1952 election took place during the Korean War, of course, heightens the parallel between that election and the one approaching. But even more striking are the similarities in public opinion during the two periods. After the Korean War began, a similar decline in satisfaction with the "way President Truman is handling his job" set in. This decline in popularity was even more pronounced in President Johnson's case, but it hasn't reached the depth to which approval of Truman had sunk. Both curves, moreover, show a tendency to level off—President Johnson, at the time he withdrew from the race, enjoyed 10 percent to 15 percent more approval than President Truman.

The polls show that the public's negative appraisal of L.B.J.'s war performance is linked to their dissatisfaction with his overall performance. President Truman likewise suffered from a critical public reaction to the way he was "handling the Korean War." In 1952, this dissatisfaction transferred to the Democratic Party and Adlai Stevenson.

Will 1968 be a replay of 1952? Surely, a complete answer to this question will depend upon the voters' response to the Paris negotiations and to the state of the union. But we already know some of the ingredients of the answer.

Let us examine the public's partisan attitudes in 1952. At that time, the Democrats drew a slight advantage from the voters' favorable evaluation of their domestic policy. They scored even better from being seen as benefiting such groups as "the working man" and "the Negro." But in the other categories—foreign policy, general performance of the party, and candidate image—the Democrats suffered badly. They suffered particularly from the combination of voters' attitudes toward foreign policy and their perception of General Eisenhower. As Campbell and his colleagues point out, "for many of his supporters, the Eisenhower appeal was very largely in terms of his presumed ability to handle [the] problem of foreign policy, specifically the Korean War. . . . The voters found it much easier to associate him favorably with their concern over the international crisis than they did Governor Stevenson. For a great many voters, it was the happy combination of the man and the hour." It is far from clear how the Democrats will rate on these factors next month. But let's review the record, as far as we know it, as it now stands.

On overall performance, since the sharp drop in favorable public opinion preceding the 1966 elections, President Johnson held a small advantage until June of 1967. Since then, he's been slightly behind. The Paris negotiations, and the limitation of the bombing of North Vietnam, reversed a two-year trend, but still not much more than 40 percent of the voters approved of the way Johnson was handling the war.

Evaluation of the President's handling of the war among Democrats has paralleled the evaluation of voters generally. However, Johnson has enjoyed about 9 percent more approval of his Vietnam performance from identifiers with his own party than from the nation. Beyond this, the response among Democrats to the changes in the war after Johnson's March 31 withdrawal speech has been more positive than past trends would have led us to expect.

It is beginning to look as if the war has become a partisan issue. That is to say, a person's approval or disapproval of the Democratic administration's Vietnam performance is more a result of that issue's being incorporated into the wider set of his partisan attitudes than of his independent assessment of the administration's performance. In this regard, it is instructive to note that, in June, while the nation at large was evenly split (41 percent: 41 percent: 18 percent) on the question of whether Vice-President Humphrey or Richard Nixon could deal better with Vietnam, 62 percent of the Democrats thought the Vice-President could do a better job, and 74 percent of the Republicans gave Nixon the nod. Apparently party identification was still quite high. We do not have the data to judge whether this is temporary, or the beginning of a trend. If it is a trend, the significance of Vietnam in the voting decision will be reduced. If it is temporary, and dissatisfaction with the Johnson administration's Vietnam performance grows (as the most recent polls indicate), we can expect a substantial number of Democrats to vote contrary to their basic party loyalty. And if the trend away from "strong" party identifications continues, we can expect the rate of defections among Democrats to go up correspondingly. Taken together, these two phenomena could compound the problem of getting Democrats who disapprove of the administration's Vietnam performance to vote for Hubert Humphrey.

The problem that Humphrey faces in attracting Independent voters who think the Vietnam issue both important and badly handled is the same as his problem with Democratic loyalists—only more so. Among Independents, the percentage approving of President Johnson's handling of the war has been about 5 percent below the national figures. This disparity carries over to judgments about whether the Vice-President could do a better job of dealing with the war. Only 35 percent of the self-styled Independents thought that Humphrey could do a better job than Nixon—six points below the national percentage. In past elections, as Tables 4 and 5 show, most Independents who thought the Republicans could do a better job in foreign policy, or who thought that the Democratic administration was responsible for a foreign-policy failure, did *not* vote Democratic.

As the situation looks now, on general and foreign-policy performance the Republicans are showing an advantage. The Democrats may again, as they did before 1964, give ground to the Republican Party in these two areas.

The images of the candidates are largely a mystery. From the Gallup Poll and our own surveys, it appears that the public is not wildly enthusiastic about either of the candidates and, more to the point, reactions to the candidates are along partisan lines.

Whether or not the state of the economy can be counted as a plus for Humphrey is a matter of controversy. Whether other components of domestic policy will continue to redound to the Democrats' advantage —considering the riots, for example—is more problematic still. But the Democrats seem to have retained their past advantage as the perceived benefactors of such groups as the aged, the black, and those with less income and those with less education.

All of this uncertainty makes prediction hazardous to the point of damn foolishness.

Our formula for voting behavior leaves us without a conclusion about the outcome next month, largely because we lack data on several of the critical factors included in that formula. This same lack of data bars a definitive conclusion on the role of the Vietnam issue. But it seems clear that "satisfaction with the way Vietnam has been handled" is the attitude whose distribution in the electorate will determine the role played by the Vietnam issue in the election. Unfortunately, direct assessment of this attitude by pollsters ceased in April.

This lack of data leaves us free to speculate about two ways that public opinion might have changed since April. On the one hand, it can be argued that the Paris negotiations improved the public's assessment of the administration's performance in Vietnam—that negotiations equal success. On the other hand, the Paris talks can be considered one of many past administration actions that only temporarily changed the direction of public opinion. Unless the Paris negotiations reach some early settlement (a cease fire, a large-scale exchange of prisoners, a stop to bombing north of the demilitarized zone coupled with an end to the shelling of Saigon), public disapproval of the administration's Vietnam performance might increase.

There is some evidence for each possibility. Before April, bombing north of the D.M.Z. was supported by most Americans. In February, we had found 46 percent of our respondents in favor of increasing the bombing and 19 percent in favor of doing what we were then doing; only 18 percent favored stopping the bombing. This distribution of opinion was virtually identical with what we found in 1967. The Gallup Poll results have paralleled our findings. This evidence would lead one to conclude that most Americans favored the bombing, and that this opinion was stable.

But in April this changed abruptly. After the President's speech, the Gallup Poll found 64 percent of

the voters supporting the decision to stop the bombing, and a substantial increase in approval of the way
the war was handled. There can be little doubt that
the onset of the Paris talks reinforced this; for at
least two years, nine Americans in ten have favored
negotiations.

The question remains whether the dramatic changes
in April will persist until November. It has happened
before. The test-ban treaty of 1963 radically reduced
the public's estimate of the likelihood of war; the
Civil Rights Act of 1964 convinced many who favored
integration that the fight was won. Dramatic policy
milestones have sometimes had a lasting effect on attitudes—symbolic content is often more important than
practical consequences.

Yet this is not always the case. It certainly was not
the case with the negotiations in the Korean War.
Negotiations began in Korea in July 1951. At that
time, the steady decline in approval of the way President Truman was handling his job was interrupted,
and for a few months public approval grew. This was
followed by an abrupt downturn, then a gradual rise
and leveling off. Negotiations were recessed in October
1952—15 months after they had begun and just before
the election. Throughout the negotiations at Panmun-
jon, although at a reduced pace, fighting continued and
casualties were suffered. We do not know which of
these elements was important as far as the 1952 election was concerned: Would the Republican margin
have been greater still if negotiations had not been
under way? Did the length of time between the onset
of negotiations and Election Day prove crucial? Did
the fact that the fighting and dying continued contribute to the Republicans' net advantage from foreign

policy?

The year 1952 is an example of the operation of the second possibility, that administration actions may have only temporary effects on the voters. The length of time since the action, and its success, are the keys to the persistence of its effects. The onset of negotiations in 1968, like other abrupt changes in the course of the war in Vietnam, led to a suspension of critical feelings. For the public, hope springs eternal—and the President appears to have a supply of "second chances" limited only by the arrival of Election Day. As the fighting continues during negotiations, we might expect a decline in public approval as the public again focuses on the results of the fighting—casualties, for example—and not the tactics by which the war is being fought at the moment.

With respect to public opinion on Vietnam, as J.S. Milstein and W.C. Mitchell have shown, four factors have been strongly related to public approval or disapproval. These are (1) our leaders' announced decision on whether to increase or decrease the war effort; (2) a similar decision on the part of North Vietnam's leaders; (3) the ratio of battle casualties on the two sides; and (4) the level of effort made by the South Vietnamese army. Over the last two years, when our leaders have taken a hard line, they have tended to lose public support; when Hanoi's leaders have taken a hard line, our leaders have tended to gain public support. When our casualties have increased relative to those of the North Vietnamese and the Vietcong, the public has responded negatively. But the public responds positively when the South Vietnamese increase their efforts. Thus, to increase support of the administration, the optimal picture would be a softening of our line, which is reciprocated by Hanoi, coupled with a drop in casualties, and the South Vietnamese taking a more active role. The Paris talks can have a great deal to do with the first three of these factors. And if the public is still assessing success and failure, the progress of the Paris talks will be reflected in the election.

But there is still a month to go before the election: What would be the likely effect of some last-minute success? While there is no direct evidence on the subject, William Caspary has shown that voters' current attitudes are strongly related to their reactions to current events, plus a "discounted" accumulation of memories of past events. This would argue that a combination of the administration's public approval at the moment, and a discounted residual of the trend, would be more strongly related to voting behavior than either factor alone. It would argue, also, that the longer a step-up in approval is delayed when the trend is downward, the greater the rise in approval will have to be if it is to overcome the cumulative effect of the downtrend.

If the "Caspary Effect" is characteristic of Vietnam opinion, the timing of any administration action (like ending the bombing of North Vietnam) would be tricky indeed. If it comes too early and does not succeed, it will contribute to the downtrend. If it comes too late for its consequences to be noted, the accumulated downtrend can outweigh the positive increment.

The role of Vietnam in the coming election is still highly uncertain. As we have seen, issues are by no means the most important determinant of the vote; rather, they take care of what's left over after party identifications have determined the decisions of most voters, and the personal qualities of the candidates have attracted many of the rest. But even after these non-issue processes have "worked their magic," there are still enough issue-voters to cause a landslide to one side or the other.

Vietnam and its domestic ramifications are *the* issues for 1968; we will know their full impact only in retrospect. After November we will know whether the unfolding of the war caused a defection from the Democratic Party of strong and weak Democrats, or whether it caused Democrats to stick and, like 1964, caused Republicans to switch. "After November" is soon enough for scientists; it will, of course, be too late for politicians.

October 1968

FURTHER READINGS SUGGESTED BY THE AUTHOR:

Domestic Sources of Foreign Policy edited by James N. Rosenau (New York: Free Press, 1967). The best compilation of what is known of the link between public opinion and foreign policy. It includes an article by Warren Miller essaying the electoral impact of foreign-policy issues.

The American Voter by Angus Campbell, Philip Converse, Warren Miller, and Donald Stokes (New York: John Wiley & Sons, 1960). This book is the classic statement of the political-social-psychological theory of voting.

Presidential Elections by Nelson W. Polsby and Aaron Wildavsky (New York: Charles Scribner's Sons, 1968). This is a highly accessible book that thoroughly describes the process of selecting and electing Presidential candidates.

The President,
the Polls, and Vietnam

SEYMOUR MARTIN LIPSET

Never before in the annals of American political history
has a President exhibited such an obvious and intense concern over his public image as indicated by the public
opinion polls. President Johnson's well-reported attention
to the rise and fall of percentage points raises the question:
what are the uses and abuses of polls in affecting the actions of political leaders.

There is a very great difference in the reliability of
responses with respect to domestic and foreign affairs.
Domestically, the polls indicate that we are dealing with
relatively stable attitudes, on issues such as the welfare state,
race relations, etc. In addition, when new issues arise such
as how to deal with inflation, unemployment, or Medicare,
people can react to them in terms of direct personal experience or liberal-conservative predispositions.

Conversely, in the area of foreign policy most Americans
know very little, and are only indirectly involved. They

have no way of checking on often conflicting reports from countries and regions under contention, nor on public sentiments elsewhere in the world. Consequently, the press and political leaders can have much more influence in determining public opinion on foreign issues than on domestic issues. Whether Tshombe is a villain or a hero, whether the downfall of Nkrumah is good or bad, is defined *for* the average American rather than *by* the average American. If we trace the poll popularity of a single leader, say Tito of Yugoslavia or de Gaulle of France, it becomes clear that the poll variations in the United States follow policy decisions made about him on the basis of whether his actions further or hamper American concerns. In other words, polls do not make policy so much as follow policy in most areas of international affairs.

When it comes to Vietnam, basically the opinion data indicate that national policy-makers, particularly the President, have an almost free hand to pursue any policy they think correct and get public support for it. They can escalate under the justification that this is the only way to prevent a "Communist take-over" in Southeast Asia; they can negotiate with the Viet Cong for a coalition government if this policy is presented as one which will gain peace while avoiding such a presumed take-over. These conclusions do not mean that most people are fickle, but rather that they agree on certain larger objectives, peace without the expansion (or contraction) of communism, and find it necessary to trust the judgment of national leaders as to what is possible given these purposes.

The highly publicized efforts by the President and other foreign policy advocates to interpret the various poll results dealing with the Vietnam conflict—with both hawks and doves claiming that the American people agree with them —point up the need to clarify the meaning of the polls. Some months ago, a faculty group at various San Francisco Bay Area colleges actually dug down in their own pockets to pay the National Opinion Research Center (NORC) of the University of Chicago to conduct a survey which might clear up some of the confusion. Unfortunately, this survey was no more conclusive than others which have been conducted over the years by other pollsters such as George Gallup, Louis Harris, National Analysts, and the Opinion Research Corporation. The results of most surveys can still be interpreted by both extremes in the foreign policy debate to fit their own preconceptions.

The truth is that the American people as a whole, and many, if not most, individuals cannot be placed in the category of dove or hawk. Two sets of attitudes stand out among the various responses. The great majority of the American people desire peace in Vietnam, do not want war with China, are prepared to accept some sort of compromise truce with the enemy, and, in fact, anticipate a negotiated peace rather than a victory which will see the defeat of the Viet Cong. On the other hand, a substantial majority is strongly hostile to communism and all the Communist countries, including Soviet Russia, Cuba, and China. Almost nobody interviewed by NORC (5 percent or less) believed that our foreign policy toward any one of these countries is "too tough"; a large majority agree with statements that the US is "too soft" in dealing with China and Cuba; almost half think we are "too soft" in our relations with the Russians. Most of those who do not think the policy is "too soft" say it is right.

Most Americans are, in fact, both doves *and* hawks; the more thorough and detailed the querying of opinions, the more clearly this appears. Early in March of this year, the Gallup Poll asked, "Would you favor or oppose bombing big cities in North Vietnam?" Sixty percent voiced opposition, while only 28 percent favored it. (The NORC study used a similar question and reported 55 percent against bombing cities in North Vietnam and 39 percent in support.) These results would seem to clearly indicate a dove majority against bombing North Vietnam. Yet in the same survey, Gallup also inquired, "Would you favor or oppose *bombing industrial plants and factories* in North Vietnam?" The response distribution was almost precisely opposite to the "bomb North Vietnamese cities" question. Sixty-one percent said they were for the bombing of factories and 26 percent were against. In other words, three-fifths of the American public were for bombing the North Vietnamese factories, but three-fifths (not all the same people) were also against bombing their cities, in March and April. This means that the policy of "strategic" bombing and avoiding "civilian" targets is generally approved. Thus, when Louis Harris asked about US resumption of bombing in January ("Do you think President Johnson was right or wrong to resume bombing in North Vietnam after the recent pause?") 73 percent said he was right; only 10 percent were opposed. And two months later a National Analysts survey conducted for NBC which inquired, "Should the US continue bombing North Vietnam?" reported almost identical results, 78 percent for continuing; 14 percent for stopping the attacks.

The American public shows a similar general propensity to discriminate among the methods which should be used in fighting the war. Almost the same size majority (68 percent) told National Analysts interviewers that they *opposed* the US using "any nuclear weapons in Vietnam," as *approved* US use of "gas that does not kill people."

Are these illogical or inconsistent responses? No, as in the case of the answers to the bombing questions, they reflect a national mood to do as little as possible to stop communist expansion. The dominant attitude seems to be not to let Vietnam "go Communist" coupled with a desire to end the war as soon as possible, on the most minimal conditions which include a willingness to negotiate directly with the National Liberation Front (NLF).

The various surveys point up this mixed pattern of responses. Peace sentiments are strong. Almost everyone (88 percent) polled by NORC would favor "American negotiations with the Viet Cong if they were willing to negotiate," and a majority (52 percent for, 36 percent against) would be willing to approve "forming a new government in which the Viet Cong took some part" in order to "end the fighting."

But the *same sample* of respondents who gave these dove answers turned into veritable militant hawks when asked, "If President Johnson were to announce tomorrow that we were going to withdraw from Vietnam and let the Communists take over, would you approve or disapprove?" Four-fifths of the NORC sample, 81 percent, disapproved, as compared with but 15 percent favoring getting out. A goodly majority (56 percent for, 39 percent against) would *not* agree to "gradually withdrawing our troops and letting the South Vietnamese work out their own problems" even though the possibility of a Communist victory was not mentioned in the question.

The willingness of the Americans to fight the war was expressed in the response to a NORC question which first asked respondents to choose among three alternative courses of action: continuing the present situation indefinitely; fighting a major war with hundreds of thousands of casualties; or supporting a withdrawal of American troops which leads to an eventual Communist take-over. Almost half (49 percent) would continue the present situation; 23 percent favored escalation to a major war; and 19 percent would support getting out. However, when the choice was narrowed to either support of escalation to a major war or withdrawal, twice as many (60 percent) chose major war as favored withdrawal. The same aggressive posture is reflected in the answers to an NBC-National Analysts poll, in March, which asked respondents to choose whether we should "pursue a more offensive ground war in Vietnam than we are presently doing, or should we establish defensive positions around the cities we now control?" Over half (55 percent) chose to escalate as compared to 28 percent who favored holding our present lines.

When pollsters' questions remind respondents of the cost of the war in lives and do not mention communism, Americans often support the more pacific alternative; when they are faced with fighting or agreeing to a Communist victory, they opt for continuing the war, and even with escalating if necessary.

Yet, though most Americans ruefully are willing to keep fighting in Vietnam if this is necessary to prevent a complete take-over, or expansion to neighboring countries, they clearly would much prefer not to be there, and are anxious and willing to turn over responsibility to someone else. Back in June 1954, when it first appeared as if the US might send troops to Indo-China, only 20 percent told Gallup interviewers that they would approve sending US soldiers "to help the French fight the Communists in Indo-China." And much more recently, on various occasions, clear majorities have reported to Gallup, Harris, and NORC alike that they would like to see the United Nations take over from the United States, either to fight or settle the war. Thus in the first few months of this year, 70 percent told NORC they would approve the UN or some neutral countries negotiating a peace "with each side holding the territory it now holds"; 74 percent indicated to Gallup interviewers they would approve the UN working out "its own formula for peace in Vietnam"; more people (49 percent) said that the US should submit the Vietnam question to the UN and abide by the UN's decision, *no matter what it is*, than opposed the idea (37 percent) ; and a UN army for Vietnam and Southeast Asia was approved by a three to one majority (almost identical to the results obtained by Gallup to a similar question a year earlier).

The strength of the sentiment to turn the war over to the United Nations may be seen in the fact that this is the only issue on which poll results indicated that negative judgments of President Johnson far outweighed his support. In September 1965, the Harris Survey reported that 42 percent agreed with the statement, the President was "more wrong than right" in not asking the UN to take over in Vietnam, while only 25 percent thought he was "more right than wrong," and the rest were not sure. A more recent Harris Survey released in early April of this year reports that Americans favor by nearly two to one (50 percent to 27 percent) "turning over the entire Vietnam war to a special three-man United Nations committee for arbitration and a decision binding on all parties."

These attitudes not only reflect ambivalent sentiments about US participation in Vietnam, they also indicate the very strong positive feeling of the overwhelming majority of the American people toward the United Nations. All the surveys have consistently indicated widespread popular support for the UN. (The vociferous rightist critics of American membership in the international body can hardly find more than a small minority to support their views among the general public. Most Americans seem to identify the UN with prospects for world peace, and are willing to do anything to endorse it, including criticizing American foreign policy if a question is worded in such a way as to make the pro-UN response involve such criticism.)

In evaluating the poll responses, it is important to keep in mind that the proportion of Americans who can be considered soft on communism is insignificantly small. Those who approve forming a new government in which the NLF takes part are almost as hard in their attitudes toward Castro, Communist China, and Russia as those who oppose NLF participation. In other words "hard line" anti-Communists are almost as prone to favor dealing with the Viet Cong directly, as those who are generally more favorable to the expansion of relations with Communist countries. For example, 60 percent of those favorable to a coalition with the Viet Cong think our policy toward Castro is "too soft," as compared with 70 percent among those who would not admit the Viet Cong to the government. The response pattern with respect to attitudes toward Communist China and Russia is similar.

What the polls show is that the anti-communism of Americans has little to do with their opinions about how the war in Vietnam should be handled at the tactical level. But, the belief in the need to defeat the Communist enemy, serves to support any actions which the President can argue need to be taken to defeat this enemy. Such attitudes provide a strong reservoir of support for the hawks, and an equally significant impediment for the doves.

These mixed "hawk-dove" sentiments in large measure underlie the general state of opinion concerning President Johnson's handling of the Vietnamese situation. Polls taken before the spring 1966 Buddhist crisis, by Gallup and Harris over the previous year, had indicated approval for the President in the ratio of two to one. The last such pre-crisis survey, Gallup's of late March, indicated that 56 percent approved, while 26 percent disapproved. (The

NORC survey taken a little earlier found a comparable division, 61 percent approving and 29 percent disapproving, almost identical to the results reported by the NBC National Analysts poll, also taken in March.)

It is difficult to tell from the available reports of the various surveys whether the critics of President Johnson are disproportionately hawks or doves. It is clear that a large majority both of the extreme hawks, those who favor "carrying the war more into North Vietnam," and of the more pacific doves, those who would "pull our troops out now," tell pollsters they oppose the President's Vietnamese policies. The President, on a number of occasions, has stated that most of those who disapprove of his Vietnamese policies are hawks, rather than doves. And he has interpreted increases in the proportions voicing criticism, such as occurred in May and June of 1966, as reflecting a growth in sentiment to escalate. This may be so, but the President has not presented figures comparing the attitudes of his supporters and opponents on a variety of specific policy issues. This would be the only way to reach a conclusion on this point.

The NORC survey tried to do so but the findings are indecisive and incomplete. Those who "disapprove the way the Johnson administration is handling the situation in Vietnam" are slightly more likely to give dove rather than hawk responses on a few policy questions. However, these data derive from those questions which produced large dove responses among the sample generally, such as negotiate with Viet Cong, form a new government with them.

Most recently, a Gallup survey taken in early June reports that among those who disapprove of Johnson's handling of the situation in Vietnam, 10 percent gave answers which could be categorized under the heading "we should be more aggressive," while 13 percent said that "we should get out." My own interpretation of the data presented by various pollsters is that the proportions of hawks and doves among the President's critics, reported recently by Gallup, has tended to be a relatively stable pattern. That is, the critics have usually contained slightly more doves than hawks. It should be stressed, however, that there is always a third group present among the President's critics whose responses cannot be classified in either category.

Clearly, the American people are worried about the Vietnam war. Indeed, they are, according to recent reports, at least twice as concerned over the war as they are over the next leading "issue"—the Negro civil rights issue. When Gallup asked a national sample in December what headline they would most like to see in "tomorrow's paper," almost nine out of ten respondents spontaneously mentioned peace. Almost half (46 percent) specifically said "peace in Vietnam," while another 41 percent stated peace in general. These findings were reiterated in the NORC study which found that more voters (62 percent) said they "worried a great deal" about the war in Vietnam than about any other issue. Only 7 percent said the issue of the war did not worry them at all.

The anxiety and serious thought which Americans devote to the Vietnamese war does not mean that they see any quick or simple way to gain the peace they so ardently desire. They know that we have not been doing well. A CBS-Opinion Research Corporation survey reported in December that when asked which side controlled "most of the land area of South Vietnam," more people said the Viet Cong. *Only 24 percent* thought the US was "making progress toward victory." The bulk of those interviewed also had a reasonably accurate estimate of the numbers of American troops in Vietnam and the casualties suffered by them. Last December, when asked by Gallup, how long they think the war will last, less than 20 percent thought it would end in a year or less; 26 percent guessed at two or three more years; while 36 percent said at least four more years. And when asked by Gallup in January of this year: "Do you think the war will end in a clear-cut victory in Vietnam, or will it end in some sort of compromise settlement?" only 7 percent foresaw a clear-cut victory; 69 percent predicted a compromise ending. This anticipation of a compromise settlement is reflected in the large majorities favoring a negotiated settlement as reported by both Gallup and Harris.

The fact that the government of South Vietnam became involved in serious troubles with its own people in the late spring should not have been too surprising to many Americans. The CBS-National Analysts survey reported in December 1965, that only 22 percent of Americans thought most South Vietnamese are loyal to their present leaders, i.e., the Ky regime. In spite of this lack of belief in popular support for the South Vietnamese government, when this same sample was asked: "Do you think we should have pulled out before American fighting units became involved, or do you think that staying there was the right thing to do?" only 20 percent said we should have pulled out, 65 percent thought staying in Vietnam was right. The ability of people to hold these contradictory beliefs is based on an overriding belief that supporting the war is not specific to Vietnam, but a necessity to stop Communist expansion.

The data presented by the various pollsters make it possible for one to argue that the American people are tough, soft, informed, confused, decisive, and indecisive, depending on the case one wants to make. To interpret them in any of these ways, however, would be wrong. These attitudes reflect certain consistent underlying beliefs about peace and Communism which most of the American public, like those who hold office, find difficult to reconcile. Very few are willing to approve actions which they perceive would increase the chances for a larger war, reduce the possibilities for early peace, or encourage Communist expansion into non-Communist areas, inside or outside of Vietnam. And the survey data suggest that most Americans share with their leaders the sense that they are in a morass from which they do not yet see a way out.

The findings of the surveys clearly indicate that the President, while having a relatively free hand in the actual decision-making to escalate or to de-escalate the war, is more restricted when considering the generic issues of action or inaction. He must give the appearance of a man *engagé,* of being certain of what he is doing, i.e., that the anticipated consequences do in fact come about.

The President seems to present his program along two parameters:

■ as part of a plan to secure the peace, particularly if the action involved is actually escalation;

■ pacific actions are presented as ways to contain communism, or even to weaken it.

The President knows that in order to get the support of the American people for a war they wish they never were in, he must continually put his "best peace foot" forward— he continually talks and offers peace, so that he may have public endorsement for war.

And conversely, any effort to make peace, to reach agreement with any Communist state, would best be presented as a way to "contain" Communism, to weaken it by facilitating splits among the various Communist states, or to help change it internally so that it will be less totalitarian, more humane, and less expansionist.

There are, of course, important limits, real limits, on the ability of the President to determine public response. During

1966, his personal popularity and endorsement for the Vietnamese policy dropped sharply—to a point where the percentage indicating support fell to less than 50 percent. A Gallup survey in May indicated only 41 percent of the general public approved "the way Johnson is handling the situation in Vietnam," as against 37 percent who disapproved. This general decline in support was a result of the internal turmoil among the South Vietnamese, and a feeling that the President had become indecisive in his handling of the war. Clearly, there was no way that the President could have prevented the American people from learning of the opposition in the streets to General Ky's government. These events, according to Gallup, led to a sizable increase in the proportion who felt that continued fighting is useless, who viewed the war as lost. Gallup reported as of early June, before the facilities at Haiphong and Hanoi were bombed, that for the first time since the US became heavily engaged in Vietnam, less than half the population, 48 percent supported continuing the war, as compared with 35 percent who were in favor of taking our troops out.

Yet according to the Harris Survey, another effect of the despair over the South Vietnamese turmoil was to increase sharply the numbers of Americans who favored sharp escalation in tactics as a means of ending the war. Thus, *before* the decision was made to bomb installations at Hanoi and Haiphong in June, Harris reported that those in favor of bombing the two cities had increased from 20 percent as of September 1965, to 34 percent in May 1966, while opposition to such bombings had dropped from 47 to 34 percent. Support for blockading North Vietnamese ports, a step not yet taken, jumped from 38 percent in September to 53 percent in May. Those willing to "carry the ground war into North Vietnam at the risk of bringing Red China into the fighting" went up from 28 percent in December 1965 to 38 percent in May.

Once the religious strife was terminated, the President could regain his hold on public opinion by the twin tactics of escalating the bombing raids and emphasizing the military defeats suffered by the Viet Cong, and the presumed demoralization of the Ho government in Hanoi. Gallup reports as of July 1966 show that between early June and mid-July general support for the President jumped from 46 percent to 56 percent and specific endorsement of his role in the Vietnam conflict rose from 41 percent to 49 percent. As of August Harris found that "more than 80 percent favor the bombings of military targets at Hanoi and Haiphong. . . ." Those in favor of intensifying the war effort rose from 47 percent in May to 60 percent in August. These changes underscore the need for Presidential action as a basis of continuing support.

These results do not mean, however, that any course of decisive action is without great political risks. The deeply felt general anxiety over the continuation and escalation of the war may result in considerable loss of support to the Democrats in the 1966 Congressional elections. A minority, but one large enough to affect the outcome in many districts, is increasingly unhappy. The fact that some of the critics are hawks and others doves, does not change the fact that they may vote for the opposition, or not vote at all as a means of protest. A Harris Survey early in the year reports that "those who disagree with the Administration conduct in Vietnam today say they are likely to vote 52-48 percent Republican next fall."

There are other indications of the diverse ways which the continuation of the war may aid the Republicans and even stimulate right-wing sentiment in the country. On one hand, in July of this year for the first time in many years, a larger group (30 percent) told Gallup interviewers that the Republicans are more likely than the Democrats (22 percent) to keep the US out of World War III. Contrast this result with the finding in October 1964 that 45 percent saw the Democrats as the more pacific party with 22 percent for the Republicans. But the survey data also suggest that the social base for a new wave of McCarthyism may be emerging. In March of this year when asked by national analysts: "Do you agree with the right of an American citizen to demonstrate against the war in Vietnam?" only 34.5 percent agreed, 62 percent opposed. Two earlier surveys, by the Opinion Research Corporation and Gallup in November and December, also yielded results which suggest that the large majority of the public do not view opposition to the war as legitimate, seeing the bulk of the protesters as "communists" or "draft dodgers."

To sum up the implications of the polls, it seems clear that the President holds the trump cards in dealing with the public on foreign policy matters. The public knows they do not know, and feel they must trust the President, for there is no one else on whom they can rely in the international field. There is no equivalent to Dwight Eisenhower around today—an opposition leader with sufficient personal status and international experience to become a counter-center of foreign policy confidence.

If this is so, why does Lyndon Johnson pay so much attention to survey results. Not, I would suspect, to convince himself that he is doing right, or that he is following the wishes of the people. *The President makes opinion, he does not follow it.* His interest in the opinion polls, therefore, reflects his desire to be sure that his approach is reaching the American public in the way he wants them affected. The polls tell him how good a politician he is. They are also a weapon against his critics. He feels he is under no obligation to make public politically unpalatable information. And, as we have seen, there is enough in the surveys for the President to find justification for whatever policy he wants to pursue in Vietnam, and to tell his political critics that the people are behind him.

The poll data can also enable the President, and other politicians as well, to ignore opposition demonstrations, which are organized by relatively small minorities. Thus, opinion surveys of university student populations, who have provided the main source of organized disagreement, indicate that the overwhelming majority of American students are behind the war. There have been four national surveys of campus opinion, two in 1965 by Louis Harris and *Playboy*, and two in 1966 by Samuel Lubell and Gallup, the latter in June. All of these indicate that a large majority of American students (between two-thirds and three-quarters) support the war in Vietnam. Faculty opinion, according to a *Playboy* poll, is also behind the war, although by a smaller majority than the students.

As a final point, it may be noted that the opposition to the Vietnamese war is far less than that voiced to the Korean war. As of January 1951, Gallup reported that 66 percent said: "Pull our troops out of Korea as fast as possible" as contrasted with 25 percent who said stay and fight. If the evidence of the polls is to be believed, the American public are far more willing to fight in Asia today than 15 years ago.

The findings presented in this effort to sum up the results of opinion surveys on the Vietnam war may depress many who hope to modify American foreign policy through mobilizing segments of the public in support of various peace movements. It is obvious that such efforts face considerable obstacles, particularly during an on-going war.

September/October 1966

American Aid
Is Damaging Thai Society

LUCIEN M. HANKS

Over 40,000 American troops are based in the South-east Asian country of Thailand. They are advising Thai soldiers fighting guerrillas, or they are flying bombing missions against North Vietnam. The United States, along with other Western powers and agencies, has given Thailand hundreds of millions of dollars, per-haps billions, in military and economic aid. While these facts may be unsettling to Americans, many of whom don't want this country involved in another Asian war, what do they mean to Thailand?

It is my contention that this military aid is upset-ting the social balance in Thailand, or at least threaten-ing it. Ordinarily we view such assistance as a stabiliz-ing force. Even critics of America's foreign aid make this assumption when they say that this aid sometimes helps unsavory regimes remain in power. But I am sug-gesting the reverse: *The volume of our military aid in*

Thailand is threatening the very order that we would preserve.

I am not directly concerned with the social disruption that surrounds American bases in Thailand. So far, the inflation, labor shortages, falling agricultural production, and rising incidence of venereal disease appear to be local, and are likely to diminish when the bases are closed. I am much more concerned with why Thailand granted permission for the United States to build foreign bases there, accepted American troops without a time-limit, and permitted the United States to use these bases for bombing neighbors not hostile to Thailand. We speak of Thailand as a nation, but this is not the way nations behave. Senator J. William Fulbright once asked Thanat Khoman, Thai Foreign Minister, if the Thai felt comfortable with these American bases. Khoman thereupon denounced him for inquiring into matters that, according to Khoman, were none of Fulbright's business. Then too, Thailand permitted Japan to build bases there in World War II, and as a consequence was severely bombed by the Allies. This disaster could not have been forgotten in 1961 when the American troops were invited into Thailand to stem a threatened invasion from Laos. Neither the establishment of Japanese nor American bases seems to have been in Thailand's "national interest," as we understand it.

Just as we can ignore "national interest" as an explanation of Thai policy, we can also bypass a host of other formulations that might account for Thai behavior. Here I refer to "public opinion," "dictatorship," "fear of Communism," "underdeveloped nation," "traditional society," and so on. If any of these apply, they do so only peripherally. In regard to "public opinion" and "fear of Communism," for example, there simply are no citizen groups ready to defend their villages and towns house by house against an invader. No mass uprising of peasants or slaves has ever occurred in Thai history. And apart from a few intellectuals, there is no public concern with political affairs or ideology.

To understand the social disequilibrium in Thailand, and to see that our military aid is bringing it about, we must first have a clear vision of Thai society and its principles of operation. Without such an understanding—and this, of course, holds true for any country where we spend our money—our most philanthropically offered aid may well prove to be a Trojan horse.

The social order of Thailand is like a bundle of fine golden chains of varying lengths, with only occasional cross-connections. Pulled taut from the end, the chains resist or move as one, but a finger passes easily between the strands. Ordinarily we think of societies as well integrated, with parts fitting into other parts, each contributing to the whole. But the Thai social order is loosely structured, and in a special way. It is loose only from side to side, not from the top or bottom.

When our team of anthropologists from Cornell University entered Bang Chan in Thailand, we expected to find an "organized village." We searched many a month for its center, for its integrating structure—without success. Bang Chan had a name, but not even the glimmering of a community. Individualism seemed to reign supreme.

A farmer, angry because he could not paddle his boat home through the low water, tried to persuade his neighbors to help him dig out the canal that meandered past all their houses. All refused.

Parents had sons become monks by sending them to study at the temple, where each student gained merit by giving alms—not to the temple, but to his priest. Only when someone wanted to gain additional merit by erecting a new building did the temples grow. Still, in all likelihood, repairs would never be made.

We met the leaders of the village, the elected headmen. These leaders faithfully attended meetings at the district office and brought back word of district business to those who wanted to hear. Some villagers sought out the headman for advice or information; but so did residents of other villages. Some householders in Bang Chan went elsewhere to get information—to avoid their own headman.

If we wanted to find out something about a given family, we went to that family. None of the neighbors knew enough to even gossip.

In short, here was a mosaic of separate households, joined only by proximity.

Now and then, there were some common undertakings, but these were not initiated by ordinary villagers but by superiors—the district officer three miles away in Minburi, or the abbot of the local temple. Thus, every year the weeds were cut and the village buildings were swept for the Water Festival. The district officer once even managed to get the canal dug deeper.

The Thai explanation of this willingness to cooperate with superiors is characteristic: "A rich man can help a poor man, but not another rich man. What can a rich man give another rich man? But a poor man needs many things." At every important step in life, some superior—in age, wealth, or position—must be present to help. Elder brothers and sisters lug their juniors around, buying them soda pop, wiping their noses, comforting them when they cry. An employer not only provides a place to work and a weekly wage, but gives extra in time of need, allows workers to use company tools for themselves, goes to the weddings and cremations, eats from the same pot, and sleeps alongside his employees in the same room.

And so did Bang Chan look upward for help from powerful figures. The more confident villagers frequented the district officer's quarters, asking for help and quickly responding to his requests. A very few dared visit the government offices in Bangkok if, perhaps, a former acquaintance worked there. The clerks, division heads, and others of the bureaucratic hierarchy usually lay far beyond their reach, so as a rule the villagers addressed only the officials nearest in status to themselves. Ministers and the King towered far above at dizzying heights.

Bang Chan's householders were linked upwards to superiors, who might be able to accomplish what the villagers as individuals could not. But a distinct distance lay between casual neighbors. Below, in the linked chain, each man had ties to his children or possibly younger siblings. The wealthier ones, as superiors, would look after a few tenant families or a hired man. These are the chains. Householders who aren't linked in—tenant farmers in search of land to work, or laborers "with only their hands"—look up for a superior to help them.

In Thai government we find the same design. Again, the individual chain is not linear; the director-general of a government department is like a parent to all his employees. Indeed, the word *mae* (mother), in compound words like *maethap* (commander-in-chief), implies devotion to many. The director-general may play cards with his assistant after hours, lend money to his deputy to finance a marriage, invite a stenographer to the beach on a weekend. In turn, these subordinates may have little to do with one another, paying heed only to their superiors and subordinates and ignoring their equals. When the director-general's father dies, word passes quickly down the chains. Automobiles are commandeered, flowers are sent to the cremation, and gifts are produced for the guests; all these services come from the people who may be completely unknown to the director-general. They have been drawn in by members of his chain, responding to the relayed call and eager to be noticed and remembered by their superiors and by the important man.

In Thailand, a chain of any length and durability survives because it has a monopolistic hold on some public service. The Bangkok electric company, which generates power for the city, furnishes a modest example. This company was started by a prince during the days of absolute monarchy. Today, with the revenues from the company, the prince's descendants care for several hundred employees and their dependents. The Customs Department has built a regulatory authority over the port of Bangkok—the only deep-water port in the country, aside from one built almost from scratch by the Pentagon for its own uses. The Customs Department thereby controls imports and exports. The tariff that a shipper pays to bring goods in or out depends upon his bargaining power, despite an official list of duties that gives an air of legal finality. Only the defenseless pay the full rate. And then there are the mammoth chains like the air force, the army, and

the Ministry of the Interior—with multiple monopolies and multiple sources of revenue.

Though Westerners regard these operations—electric power, customs, the army—as public services, in
Thailand they are like concessions earning their own
way. In fact, anyone who wants the police to make an
investigation must pay the price the police ask for their
services. These monopolies, after all, can count on the
Ministry of Finance to give them only a small part of
the money they need. Even if fairly collected from rich
and poor alike, public tax receipts would not come near
producing the income needed to support the luxurious
living of many officials. Each chain, therefore, enjoys
its own special sources of revenue. Thus, a local police
department will barricade certain roads and derive its
revenues from passing busses and trucks. On this income the police will live, and the greater the take the
better the living. Some chains can provide goods and
clothing at reduced prices, free transportation, housing,
credit at diminished interest rates, and possibly even
vacations and amusements. One needs only be linked
into the chain through friends or relatives who own
or operate markets, banks, or summer resorts.

The presence of a Civil Service Commission, comp-
troller-general, and Ministry of Finance need not deceive us, for they, too, instead of performing only a
specialized public service, represent, respectively, monopolies on new personnel, on the use of funds, and
on the collection of taxes. Only a weak department
must operate at the basic salary rate specified by the
civil service, and many kinds of personnel never even
take a civil-service examination.

Between these monopolistic chains, relations vary—
from indifference through guarded deals to outright

hostility. The Ministry of Agriculture has little to do with the Ministry of Education, though both occupy almost adjacent buildings and both operate universities. Elsewhere, the Department of Public Welfare rather coolly cooperated with the Department of Irrigation in moving villages to high grounds during the building of a new dam—the public-welfare department claims to have been pulled in when irrigation officials could not cope with moving an entire community.

The feints and blows of active battle between chains generally escape public gaze, yet the general outlines of attack and defense are clear. For example, a man who obtained land in a mountainous area found his claim threatened by the Department of Forestry. This department sought the land without compensation. The owner, by making deals with superiors, brought the case to the cabinet level for arbitration. His lease was confirmed only after he made a palliating payment to the forestry department.

On the streets of Bangkok, the debris of intra-governmental battles is clearly visible. Down along the Chao Phraya River, the Ministry of Cooperatives, born in 1953, languishes in a few offices next to the fish market: Stronger chains have snatched away its support, and over the years it has shrunk in size and authority. On another street a vacant mansion with a handsome gate stands without a visitor, although it was the headquarters of Prime Minister Phibul Songkram's political party, which dissolved at the moment of his hasty departure from the country in the coup of 1957. Then again, during this era the navy was so weak a chain that only one minesweeper could be put to sea. The navy was paying the penalty for its complicity in the unsuccessful coup d'état of 1949. Its conduct had been unforgivable. After inviting Prime Minister Phibul for a reception aboard a cruiser, navy officers had tried to hold him prisoner as they ran down the river toward the sea. Luckily he jumped overboard and swam ashore unharmed, but he did order the bombing of that cruiser by the air force. Today, with a new cabinet and with U.S. aid, the 71-vessel Thai navy cruises the Pacific and fights for the allies in Vietnam.

Finally, we must beware of assuming that a chain is linked together because of feudal loyalty. Only as long as a superior is satisfied with a dependent, and a dependent can find no better alternative, are the two linked together. In Thailand, no obligation outlives its peculiar advantages; guilt and remorse do not enter human relations. Indeed, a good-hearted employer gains in esteem by helping his employee find better work elsewhere, for employers, too, are always looking for a superior who offers greater rewards. Even in government circles, one returns after a few years of absence to find strangers behind familiar desks. Chains are continuously being linked anew as the fortune of one person declines and that of another ascends.

These autonomous monopolies in Thailand have to be linked together if only to cope with the novelties of each succeeding day. And the authority for linking these great chains is at the top: Cabinet ministers are spokesmen for their chains. Confrontation between powerful predators is dangerous, however, and the weak need defenders against the strong, while the strong have to be restrained. Therefore, weaker chains unite with stronger ones against the mighty until a balance is struck, the mighty confronting the mighty. Then various *quid pro quo* deals are made that form

126 of 192 / LUCIEN M. HANKS

the cabinet and enable it to meet new issues with deli-
cate shifts that sustain the balance. The Prime Minister
sometimes works as if he were the driver of two strong
horses, physically weaker than either yet able to help
all reach their destination. Then again he may lead,
like the strongest and most agile horse in the herd.

There were times when the King, as head of a single chain, guided the country. This arrangement
seemed quite stable. Yet since the ending of absolute
monarchy in 1932, the palace has remained apart from
the political arena, a separate chain with untried
strength drawn from the crown properties and from its
sacred aura. Since King Phumiphol Aduldet's ascent
to the throne in 1949, he has rarely even commented
on the state of the nation. But the throne is not to be
ignored. Most ministries render some service to the
crown, be it ever so slight, providing manpower for
the palace guards, or men and equipment to build the
new palace. In turn, ministers call upon His Majesty
to open public buildings and to dignify their anni-
versaries.

If the Thai social order is a bundle of fine golden
chains, let us spread them flat to observe the connections. They appear linked tentatively in balance at the
center and fanning out in all directions like the spokes
of a wheel. The longest chains, like those of the King
and the Prime Minister, extend into paddy fields perhaps owned by the Crown or the Prime Minister's
brother. One may find occasional shorter lengths that
are unattached—say, an old provincial land-holding
family—but to protect its holdings the head would be
well advised to seek a patron. Then, at the periphery,
are many small connections varying from one to ten
links. These shifting poor people join chains, but since

they make minimal contributions they are easily snipped off at the first sign of hard times.

The shifting of attachments to other chains occurs most frequently at the periphery, but can be found at all points. Some quasi-private company breaks away from the chain of the Ministry of Finance and becomes attached to the Ministry of National Development. At the cabinet level, such shifts move great chains along their entire length. One may hear continuous rustling as the golden links separate and rejoin at new points.

Thus, the government presents itself in familiar guise but acts in unfamiliar ways. No jurisdictional boundaries divide the public from the private interest, or firmly distinguish between functions. What Westerners abhor as corruption forges the very links of the society: Gifts or favors are granted in return for benefits. Where we expect coordination, as between specialized budget-makers and determiners of policy, great gaps appear. Where we expect separation of function, as between commerce and government, a firm union has been welded. Here I would recapitulate three characteristics of these chains: (1) their monopolistic character, (2) their potential for breaking and reuniting at any point along their entire length, and (3) the necessity for balance, which enables some coordination of the whole.

Economic aid from the United States to Thailand began in the early 1950s and then mounted steadily. In addition, other international agencies—the World Bank, the United Nations, and the Columbo Plan—contributed grants and loans. Over the years the United States contributed between one-third and two-thirds of Thailand's total foreign economic aid. These funds were assigned to variety of projects under several ministries and departments. Highways were built, dams constructed, new crops tested, and parasitic diseases reduced. Certain agreements extended the projects for a few years, but for the most part the funds terminated when each project was completed. Many donors were involved with many recipients, the period of the relationship was short-lived, and the sums involved in the projects were relatively small. Thus, these sources of revenue did not strengthen any single chain, so the equilibrium between chains could be maintained by compensatory adjustments.

But military aid, particularly in the past five years, has meant that large sums went to a very *few* people. Unfortunately, information about this expenditure of hundreds of millions of dollars is confidential. I therefore rely on a series of impressions.

Judging by the headquarters of the Joint U.S. Military Advisory Group in 1954, the beginning was modest. Ten years later, in 1964, the company-sized headquarters had become fit for a regiment, and operated branches in many parts of the country as well. Then too, naval facilities at the port of Bangkok had been renewed and expanded; ships from the Thai navy were cruising the sea. The air-force fields and planes had been increased, not only at Don Muang but at many other parts of the country. If military expenditures did not exceed the economic and technical expenditures, they were certainly equal—and flowed from the same sources principally to the Thai army, navy, and air force, with small amounts going to the police.

Viewed from Bangkok, with Thai habits of thinking, the Pentagon has linked itself as patron to the military chains. Field marshals, air marshals, and admirals have placed themselves in a position to accept direction from their benefactor. Unlike the Americans, the Thai recipients are concerned neither with chip-on-shoulder autonomy nor with interference in their private affairs. These men, trained by their social order, gratefully accept the largess of a superior, and eagerly turn it to the use of their dependents. In these circumstances, what the superior wishes is a dependent's amiable duty to provide, for to raise questions threatens the integrity of the chains. Thus, when Washington proposes to build air fields, to man them with Americans, and subsequently to fly bombers from the fields for the Vietnamese war, the Thai military cannot resist. When Robert Shalpin recently questioned a Thai general about the use of the air bases, he was told, "I am just a hotel keeper who rents out rooms. I do not care what my guests do in the rooms or who they invite up there." The general shuts his eyes and puts his faith in his superior, as any self-respecting Thai must do in these circumstances.

As a result of this relationship with the Pentagon, the military has grown at the expense of other chains. At the cabinet level, Prime Minister Thanom Kittikachorn and his military leaders appear to be pitted against an array of civilian ministers. Let us recapitulate the signs of the struggle. In 1965 the Minister of the Interior, a member of the military alliance, ordered elementary-school teachers to report to representatives of his ministry throughout the kingdom. He justified this order on grounds of administrative efficiency. By appropriating the entire elementary-school system, the Minister of the Interior reduced the personnel in the chain of the Ministry of Education. The Ministry of Education was unable to defend itself. Shortly thereafter began a series of assassinations of schoolteachers, especially in the northeast. The public spokesmen attributed the murders to "Communist infiltrators." Yet the assassinations took place in many parts of the northeast, and Communist insurgents had been found in only one province. Of course, no one has been able to establish that the dead teachers resisted transfer to the Ministry of the Interior, or to find direct evidence of police complicity in these murders. Nevertheless, so much ill-will accumulated on the local level that Police General Prasert Richirawongse warned provincial policemen to "stop causing trouble to people through extortion and unfair treatment. If local Thai officials did not cause trouble, there would be no Communist-led insurgency." Whether or not Thai provincial officials actually provoked disorders in order to lure additional support from Communist-sensitive Washington must remain a conjecture. Nonetheless, American military aid—in transporting Thai troops and in detecting subversion—came to the rescue.

Intra-governmental tensions appear to have developed within the cabinet also over the building and manning of the air fields by American troops. Unlike the open welcome of the American soldiers in 1961 to prevent Communist insurgency from Laos, subsequent military operations were kept officially secret. When these operations became known, it fell not to the military but to the Ministry of Foreign Affairs, staffed mainly by princes and sons of former aristocrats, to explain to the international public. Instead of a suave and articulate defense of his country, Foreign Minister Khoman replied with irritation to Senator Fulbright's inquiries about these bases. He had not asked for U.S. troops, he said, and if necessary they could be withdrawn. This statement contrasts not only with the usual tenor of diplomatic language, but with the attitude of the Thai army general who compared himself to a hotel keeper. Uneasiness seems apparent.

Uneasiness is also suggested in King Phumiphol's address to a group of students at Thammasat University. Though the King rarely comments on governmental affairs, on this occasion he said, "If all corrupt persons were executed, there might not be many persons left. I am at my wits' end to know how to remedy it." According to private reports, the King is deeply troubled by the imbalance caused by the mounting military operations, and he fears being forced to abdicate. His veiled attack on the military roused Pote Sarasin, the civilian Minister of National Development, to propose a law barring officials, including generals, from secondary jobs with Thailand's state enterprises. As another result of the King's attack, one general resigned from the Bangkok port authority, and a second was sentenced to prison for extortion.

A further sign of civilian counterattack is the announcement that the U.S. government will provide private aid to guarantee Thai agriculture against loss. Though governments have attempted to promote the flow of private capital into foreign countries, never before has an American government underwritten a private foreign investor against losses. Thus, private American investors have entered Thailand to help counter the imbalance from the growth of military chains. Though only $3 million is involved in this particular agreement, Washington is apparently becoming aware of the effects of its military presence.

Yet I wonder whether Washington is aware of the

other risks. The very size of the present aid is corroding the integrity of the chains. Highly placed recipients, like the late Prime Minister Sarit Thanarat, open new accounts at Swiss banks and buy luxurious mansions for their mistresses instead of passing funds along to the more integral parts of their chain of dependents. A reduction in U.S. aid, of course, would lead to quick dissolution of the chains, affecting first the links at the farthest periphery. These unattached little people then become the first available to insurgent leaders, whose presence quickly sets the Communist alarm clanging in Washington. New American appropriations restore stability, perhaps, but not quite the old way. Each year, old appropriations buy a little less. Inflation has set in, and the loyalty that the United States once bought for a few propeller planes now requires an airport and naval base. Tomorrow's price will be higher, and less effective in buying security.

October 1968

FURTHER READINGS SUGGESTED BY THE AUTHOR:

Bandkuad, A Community Study in Thailand by Howard Kaufman (Locust Valley, N.Y.: J.J. Agustin, 1960). A simply written and well-documented description of a rural community in central Thailand.

Politics in Thailand by David A. Wilson (Ithaca, N.Y., Cornell University Press, 1962). A search for the power centers, with particular attention on political structures and parties.

Mao
and the Death of the Revolution

ROBERT JAY LIFTON

We do well to recognize our ignorance of China. That ignorance has been perpetuated by two decades of virtual absence of either diplomatic or journalistic contact between the United States and China—a situation that, in the not too distant future, will surely be regarded as a historical oddity of the mid-20th century.

It is nonetheless possible that we have become too accustomed to a stance of ignorance. For a good deal of significant information has been reaching us—from people coming out of China, from the official press and radio, and from a great variety of semiofficial and unofficial writings and speeches (including the celebrated "great-character posters" of the Cultural Revolution)—as recorded by an international coterie of China-watchers, many of them very well informed, whose numbers ever increase. Could it be, then, that our ignorance has to do not so much with "facts" alone as with an inability to make sense of the vast amount

133

of information we do possess? What I am suggesting is that a good part of our ignorance is conceptual.

Indeed, how is one to make sense of the extraordinary events that occurred in 1966 and 1967 as part of the Great Proletarian Cultural Revolution?

There have been, in Hong Kong and elsewhere throughout the world, thoughtful approaches to an understanding of the Cultural Revolution. These have stressed such factors as China's (and especially Mao's) "Yenan Syndrome" or "Complex," the nostalgia for the heroic revolutionary methods and achievements of days gone by; China's abrupt loss of a comfortable relationship to her own cultural past; her sense of mounting threat from the outside, especially from America's intervention in Vietnam; and her undergoing a kind of "Protestant-Catholic dispute" between evangelical reawakening and established bureaucratic compromise. All of these interpretations contain considerable truth, and the first in particular illuminates much of what has been occurring. But we have lacked a general perspective within which to comprehend both psychological motives and historical context—that is, a psychohistorical framework.

I should like to suggest that much of what has been taking place in China recently can be understood as a quest for revolutionary immortality. By revolutionary immortality I mean a shared sense of participating in permanent revolutionary fermentation, and of transcending individual death by "living on" indefinitely within this continuing revolution.

Central to this point of view is the concept of symbolic immortality: of man's need, in the face of inevitable biological death, to maintain an inner sense of continuity with what has gone on before and what will go on after his own individual existence. From this point of view the sense of immortality is much more than a mere denial of death; it is part of compelling, life-enhancing imagery binding each individual person to significant groups and events removed from him in place and time. It is the individual's inner perception of his involvement in what we call the historical process. The sense of immortality may be expressed biologically, by living on through (or in) one's sons and daughters and their sons and daughters; theologically, in the idea of a life after death or of other forms of spiritual conquests of death; creatively, through "works" and influences persisting beyond biological death; through identification with nature, and with its infinite extension into time and space; or experientially, through a feeling-state—that of experiential transcendence—so intense that, at least temporarily, it eliminates time and death.

While this may at first seem a rather abstract approach to the passions and actions of old revolutionaries and young followers, I believe that only by recognizing such life-and-death components of the revolutionary psyche can we begin to comprehend precisely these passions and actions.

Applying these modes of symbolic immortality to the revolutionary, we may say that he becomes part of a vast "family" reaching back to what he perceives to be the historical beginnings of his revolution and extending infinitely into the future. This socially created "family" tends to replace the biological one as a mode of immortality; moreover, it can itself take on an increasingly biological quality, as, over the generations, revolutionary identifications become blended with national, cultural, and racial ones. The revolutionary denies theology as such, but embraces a secular utopia through images closely related to the spiritual conquest of death and even to an afterlife. His revolutionary "works" are all important, and only to the extent that he can perceive them as enduring can he achieve a measure of acceptance of his own eventual death. The

natural world to which he allies himself is one that must
be transformed by revolution while continuing to contain
all that revolution creates. And his experiential transcendence can approach that of religious mystics, as a glance
at some of the younger participants in China's Cultural
Revolution confirms.

What all this suggests, then, is that the essence of the
"power struggle" taking place in China, as of all such
"power struggles," is power over death.

Central to China's recent crisis, I believe, is a form of
anxiety related to both the anticipated death of a great
leader and the "death of the Revolution" he has so long
dominated. This death anxiety is shared by leader and
followers alike, but we do best to focus for a time upon
the former.

It is impossible to know Mao's exact physical or mental
state. But let us assume, on the basis of evidence we have,
that the 74-year-old man has generally been vigorous, that
he has experienced rather severe illness in recent years,
and that he has always been a man of strong revolutionary
passions. We can go a bit further, especially on the basis
of a valuable interview with him conducted in January
1965 by Edgar Snow, perhaps the American who over the
years has been closest to Mao.

Snow found Mao alert, "wholly relaxed," and impressive
in his stamina during their four-hour meeting. He also
found him "reflecting on man's rendezvous with death and
ready to leave the assessment of his political legacy to
future generations." Indeed, Snow's general description of
the interview suggests a man anticipating, if not preoccupied
with, death. Snow reports Mao as having said that "he was
going to see God." And when Snow responded by reassur-
ing Mao that he seemed to be in good condition that
evening,

"Mao Tse-tung smiled wryly and replied that there was perhaps some doubt about that. He said again that he was getting ready to see God very soon."

We need not dwell on Mao's rather striking use of the theological idiom, other than attributing it to a combination of playfulness and perhaps an unconscious inclination— on the part of a man who early in his life had renounced rural supernatural beliefs in favor of Marxist-scientific ones —to hedge his bets a little. When Snow questioned him on the matter, he denied any belief in a diety, but observed rather whimsically that "some people who claimed to be well informed said there was a God. There seemed to be many gods and sometimes the same god [when called forth for self-serving political purposes] could take all sides."

More important from our standpoint are the reminiscences that immediately follow—about family members who had died, about his career as a revolutionary, and about the "chance combination of reasons" that had caused him to become interested in the founding of the Chinese Communist Party. Involved here is an old man's nostalgic need to review his past life in relationship to his forthcoming death. That is, death is seen as a test of the quality of one's overall existence. And in the face of a threat of total extinction one feels the need to give form to that existence—to *formulate* its basic connectedness, its movement or development, and above all its symbolic integrity or cohesion and significance.

Prominent among these reminiscences is Mao's sense of being an eternal survivor—his recollections of both his brothers having been killed, of the execution of his first wife during the Revolution, and the death of their son during the Korean War. Mao commented that it was "odd" that he had escaped death, that "death just did not seem to want" him. He described several narrow escapes, including one in which he was "splashed all over with the blood of another soldier," but he always emerged unscathed.

Mao seems to be telling us that his death is both imminent and long overdue. What he considers remarkable is not that so many family members and revolutionary comrades (the two categories become virtually inseparable) have died around him but that he has in each case been spared. We recognize the survivor's characteristically guilt-laden need to contrast his own continuing life with others' deaths.

For Mao is surely the survivor par excellence, the hero of a truly epic story of revolutionary survival, that of the Long March of 1934-1935, in which it is believed that more than 80 percent of the original group perished along a 6,000-mile trek in order that the remainder—and the Revolution itself—might stay alive. To transcend his guilt, the survivor must be able to render significant the death immersions he has experienced—and, in Mao's case, done much to bring about. This kind of survivor formulation faces both ways: justification of the past and contribution to the future.

Thus, for a man in Mao's position—of his age and special commitments—the affirmation of a sense of immortality becomes crucial. The overwhelming threat is not so much death itself as the suggestion that his "revolutionary works" will not endure.

We sense the passion behind his apparent calm as he goes on, during the same interview, to describe the "two possibilities" for the future: first, the "continued development of the Revolution toward Communism"; and second, "that youth could negate the Revolution and give a poor performance: make peace with imperialism, bring the remnants of the Chiang Kai-shek clique back to the mainland, and take a stand beside the small percentage of counter-revolutionaries still in the country." The first is an image of continuous life; the second of death and extinction, of impaired immortality. What he said next—"Of course he did not hope for counterrevolution. But future events would be decided by future generations . . ."—is unexpectedly stark in its suggestion of negative possibility. He is, in other words, far from certain about the fate of his revolutionary works, about the vindication of his own life.

Mao's ultimate dread—the image of extinction that stalks him—is the death of the Revolution. When he speaks of the possible "poor performance" of the young, his overriding concern is that the immortal revolutionary legacy will be squandered. As he pointed out to Snow in that same interview, "those in China now under the age of 20 have never fought a war and never seen an imperialist or known capitalism in power." His fear is not simply that the young are too soft, but that they may be incapable of sharing and perpetuating the world view that created the Revolution. For that world view was based upon his and his generation's specific experience, and as he goes on to say about the young, "They knew nothing about the old society at first hand. Parents could tell them, but to hear about history and to read books was not the same thing as living it." That is, in such unknowing hands the sacred thing itself—the Revolution—could be abused, neglected, permitted to die.

Such "historical death" can, for the revolutionary, represent an "end of the world," an ultimate deformation and desymbolization. It may cause anxiety similar to or even greater than that associated with the idea of individual death. Actually, the two forms of death anxiety become inseparable: If the Revolution is to be extinguished, the dying revolutionary can envision nothing but the total extinction of his own self.

Maoists repeatedly call upon certain specific images to suggest the danger of the death of the Revolution. These include "American imperialism," "feudalism," "the capitalist road," "bourgeois remnants," and "modern revisionism." American imperialism is the ultimate enemy to which one must be alert, lest is destroy the Revolution through power or guile. But the threat it poses is external and therefore largely visible. Feudal or capitalist and bourgeois remnants, on the other hand, are doubly dangerous because, as retained internal poisons whose effects are mainly upon the mind, they tend to be invisible. They thus require constant psychic purging, as provided by the extensive programs of thought reform (or "brainwashing") so long prominent in Chinese Communist practice. But what has recently emerged as the greatest threat of all is modern revisionism. For it is both an external danger, as embodied by a visible friend-turned-enemy, the Soviet Union, and an internal one of an insidious personal nature. It is a form of degeneracy or inner death experienced by those who once knew the true path to revolutionary immortality but, through a combination of moral weakness and shadowy conspiracy, strayed from it. Much more than the other negative images, modern revisionism looms as almost an immediate possibility.

But why now? Why the current crisis in revolutionary immortality? There is much evidence that the Cultural Revolution represents the culmination of a series of conflicts surrounding totalistic visions and national campaigns, of an increasing inability to fulfill the visions or achieve the transformations of the physical and spiritual environment claimed by the campaigns. The conflicts took on great intensity over the decade including the late 1950s and early 1960s, and found their quintessential expression in what was surely the most remarkable campaign of all prior to the Cultural Revolution, the Great Leap Forward of 1958.

The Great Leap Forward was a heroic attempt to achieve rapid industrialization and collectivization by making extensive use of the bare hands and pure minds of the Chinese people. Its massive failures resulted in overwhelming death imagery in several ways. It produced widespread confusion and suffering even as the regime was announcing its brilliant achievements. And its extensive falsification of statistics reached down, it was later learned, to virtually every level of the Party cadre. This falsification represented something more than merely a conscious attempt on the part of the regime to deceive the outside world: It was an expression of a powerful need (dictated by pressures from above but by no means limited to government leaders) to maintain a collective image of revolutionary vitality that became, so to speak, more real than reality itself. Such visions of transformation had become so basic to Chinese Communist (and more specifically Maoist) practice—and in many cases had been so brilliantly realized—that they could not be abandoned without a sense that the fundamental momentum of the Revolution, its life force, was ebbing. When the disparity between vision and experience became manifest, we suspect, earlier confidence in China's revolutionary immortality must have been severely undermined even among those close to Mao who had in the past shared most enthusiastically in his vision. Whether one attributed the Great Leap's failure to insufficient revolutionary zeal (as Mao did) or to an excess of the same (as did Liu Shao-ch'i and other "pragmatists"), all came to feel anxious about the life of the Revolution.

The regime's subsequent (1961-1962) economic backtracking and cultural liberalization, apparently implemented by the pragmatists despite Maoist resistance, also contributed to these conflicts. Measures deemed necessary for national recovery encouraged precisely the kinds of personal freedom and self-interest readily viewed within Chinese Communist ideology as decadent "individualism" and "economism." That is, liberalization posed a severe threat to the totalistic vision of absolute subjugation of self to regime upon which the overall claim to revolutionary immortality had been built. The same pattern had occurred before, following the Hundred Flowers episode of 1956-1957, an even more celebrated program of relaxation strongly influenced by Khrushchev's revelations about Stalin, by the Hungarian uprising, and by economic difficulties in China itself. At that time the Chinese shared in the general shattering of the image of infallibility surrounding the Soviet Union as the center of world Communism, and this must also have raised questions about their own mode of revolutionary immortality.

The liberalization of 1961-1962, following several years of economic strain and general unrest caused by the failure of the Great Leap, did not produce quite the luxuriant across-the-board condemnation of the regime that took place at the time of the Hundred Flowers. But there was nevertheless a muted historical repetition. More important, precisely the things said by many intellectuals during 1961-1962—the demand for a deemphasis of politics and for stress upon learning for its own sake (including greater use of books and equipment from capitalist countries), and especially the mockery of the regime's claim to infallibility —came to be denounced later as signs of "degeneracy" and "decay." The very fruits of liberalization became, for Mao and certain other Chinese leaders, death-tainted threats to the immortal revolutionary vision.

During the pre-Cultural Revolution decade Mao encountered increasing opposition because of his long commitment to the kind of heroic but unrealizable vision that reached its zenith in the Great Leap Forward. From at least 1955 on, the "pragmatists" (and one must always look upon the term as relative) within the Party have sought to moderate this vision and to pursue programs resembling the less militant Soviet example. They apparently succeeded in curbing Mao's influence, at least temporarily, during the late 1950s and early 1960s. This resistance to Mao, leading to his resignation under pressure from the State Chairmanship in December 1958 (though he did retain Chairmanship of the Party throughout), could take shape only because of the growing conviction that alternatives to his policies were absolutely necessary for economic and social stability. But Mao was later to refer scornfully to such pragmatists as "women with bound feet" and to associate their caution with remnants of the "dying old regime." To Mao and his supporters both his partial ouster and the programmatic alternatives of his opponents were expressions of betrayal of the revolutionary vision, evidences of death and deterioration.

Maoists later called forth the picturesque idiom of Chinese folklore to place these critics in the center of a demonology—referring to them as "demons," "devils," "monsters," "ogres," "ghosts," and "freaks." But demonology always addresses itself to the management of life and death, and includes an implicit theory of what might be called negative immortality: incarnations of evil that never die out, whatever one does to counter their nefarious influences. Groups like the Maoists that so boldly defy human limitation are inevitably plagued in turn by images of supernatural enemies. For demonology also reflects unacceptable subterranean conflicts. The "devils" and "monsters" under attack are largely inner doubts of Maoist accusers concerning their own omnipotence; they are in effect anti-immortals.

What are some of these deadly influences? Much of the

rhetoric during the Cultural Revolution and the Socialist
Education Movement preceding it had been a reaction and
an answer to ideas expressed during the preceding year of
liberalization (1961-1962). Under attack at the philosophical level have been theories of "human nature" along
with expressions of "humanism" (or even "socialist humanism") making their way to China from Russian and Eastern
European intellectual circles. For such concepts deny that
class origin is the ultimate moral and psychological determinant of behavior, the first by insisting that certain characteristics are shared by all mankind, and the second through
a principle the Chinese contemptuously term "love for all
people," under which even capitalists and landlords become
worthy of sympathy.

Ideas like these are dangerous because they could undermine the Maoist vision of revolutionary immortality by
encouraging people to revert to alternative intellectual tra-
ditions that extol quests for truth and self-realization. Or in
the somewhat more pejorative language of the Cultural
Revolution, they lead to desires "to get on by politics, be
really good at your specialty, and have a good life." These
ideas emerge from post-Stalinist thought, from "modern
revisionism," and express a rediscovery of the individual.
But in Chinese media they are dismissed as a "philosophy
of survival." Paradoxically, a humanist principle of "love
for all people" becomes associated (in Maoist terminology)
with "degeneration" into a "petrifying bourgeoisie," with
traits that deserve to be "relegated to the morgue." Humanist principles extolling man's life are now seen as agents of
death, as demons that must be exorcised lest their emanations destroy all.

The Chinese have also had to cope with a more concrete
form of death anxiety, stimulated by the war in Vietnam
and the fear of war with America. There is good evidence

that the repeated characterization of America as a "paper tiger" by no means eliminates in Chinese minds images of annihilation associated with America's destructive power. And Mao has in the past regularly instituted large-scale programs of reform and "rectification" when preparing for actual military combat. But I believe that the fear of war with America is in itself less of a fundamental source of the Cultural Revolution than an aggravating factor in the overall death anxiety surrounding it. And the Cultural Revolution itself appears to be more a quest for a collective sense of revolutionary power than an actual mobilization of military power to combat an outside enemy.

China's crisis, then, involves a profound general threat to revolutionary immortality intertwined with the anxious concern of an aging, partly infirm leader-hero about his capacity, through his revolutionary contributions, to outlive himself. The explosive disruption of a unified revolutionary vision (granting that conflict underlay such unity even in the past) has enormous significance as both cause and effect. For in the absence of such a vision, each individual self becomes vulnerable to the anxiety of extinction associated both with biological death and with collective forms of desymbolization. No wonder that elements of the historical past—of both Chinese tradition and the modern encounter with the West—taken on newly ominous qualities. Ghosts and demons must be slain again and again as fear for the life of the Revolution becomes associated with fear of the dead. To remain calm, to act with measure in the face of such a threat, can be perceived as an intolerable form of inactivation and stasis. The psychological stage is reached in which one cannot dispense with one's hatred. One cannot give up one's enemies.

The activist response to symbolic death—or to what might be called unmastered death anxiety—is a quest for

rebirth. One could in fact view the entire Cultural Revolution as a demand for renewal of Communist life. It is,
in other words, a call for reassertion of revolutionary immortality.

Mao seems to have an inclusive view of human culture,
but unlike Western anthropologists he feels compelled to
regulate its tone and content, at least within his nation, and
to take steps to alter it radically when it seems to be moving
in undesirable directions. A cultural revolution anywhere
involves a collective shift in the psychic images around
which life is organized. In Maoist China, however, it has
meant nothing less than an all-consuming death-and-rebirth
experience, an induced catastrophe together with a prescription for reconstituting the world being destroyed.

The "total mobilization of faith" (in Mark Gayn's
phrase) involved in this prescription for rebirth has been
peculiarly autistic. For more than a year the Chinese turned
in upon themselves, performing actions required by their
inner states or those of their leaders, however inappropriate
or repugnant these actions may have seemed to a perplexed
and fascinated outside world. In this sense the Cultural
Revolution moves in the direction of what I propose to call
psychism—the attempt to achieve control over one's external environment through internal or psychological manipulations, through behavior, determined by intrapsychic needs,
no longer in touch with the actualities of the world one
seeks to influence.

The agents of this attempted rebirth, the Red Guards,
reveal much about its nature. The tenderness of their years
—they have included not only youths in their early 20s or
late teens but children of 13 and 14—has been striking to
everyone, and then much too quickly attributed to political
necessity alone. The assumption here is that, having alienated most of the more mature population by his extreme

policies, Mao had no choice but to call upon the young. But I believe that one must look beyond such explanations (whatever their partial truth) to the wider symbolism of the Red Guard movement. The Red Guards themselves were heralded as young people who had "declared war on the old world." But in their attack upon old age and decay they were, psychologically speaking, declaring war upon death itself.

From this standpoint the August 18, 1966, rally launching the Red Guard becomes a momentous historical occasion. Western viewers of an official film of the event shown in Hong Kong and elsewhere were so impressed with the intensity of mass emotion and primal unity evoked that they have compared it with *The Triumph of the Will,* the Nazis' famous film of Hitler at Nuremberg. One of these observers, Franz Schurmann—noting the extraordinary dawn scene of a million people gathered in the great square singing "The East Is Red," Mao Tse-tung powerful in his presence though walking slowly and stiffly (and thereby encouraging rumors of severe illness), then moving out among the masses on the arm of a teenage girl—went further and spoke of the formation of a "new community." I would suggest that this new community, in a symbolic sense, is a *community of immortals*—of men, women, and children entering into a new relationship with the internal revolutionary process. An event of this kind is meant to convey a blending of the immortal cultural and racial substance of the Chinese as a people with the equally immortal Communist Revolution.

The Red Guards' symbolic mission was to "kill" virtually everything in order to clear the path for national rebirth. Hence the wide range and often remarkable targets of Red Guard activism, especially during the summer and fall of 1966: the invasion of homes, with confiscation of furniture and other possessions; the humiliation of inhabitants by verbal and sometimes physical abuse, including the ritual of parading them through the streets in dunce caps; the attacks upon temples and churches and the destruction of religious art objects as well as a certain amount of traditional and contemporary (Western-influenced) art; the cutting of hair and removing of leather shoes of Hong Kong visitors, removal from shop windows of clothes considered to be of "queer and alien fashion" even when Chinese-made, and the destruction of foreign-made objects of all kinds, including dolls and playing cards; the replacement of usual burial ceremonies with simple cremation; and the demand that traffic signals be reversed so that red have the properly positive connotation of "go," that the order in military drill be changed from "eyes right" to "eyes left," and that Peking itself be renamed "The East Is Red." Those victimized were accused of being "vampires" and made to ring "death bells." In this way alleged evil is linked with death. The "enemy" is defined as "whoever denies or is opposed to the proletarian [Maoist] line of our Party," followed by the simple statement: "He will die and we will live!" Beyond the simple threat, we encounter in this last expression a fundamental psychological impetus for victimization (or what is more gently called "prejudice"): the need to reassert one's own immortality, by contrasting it with its absence in one's victim.

Only Mao and his thought were to remain as the source of rebirth. The man and his words have fused into a powerful image, which has become the essence of revolutionary immortality as well as the energizer for its quest.

This is by no means the first time that a political leader has been made into a divinity. But few in the past could have matched Mao in the superlatives used, the number of celebrants, or the thoroughness with which the message of glory has been disseminated. Even more unique has been the way in which the leader's words have become vehicles for elevating him, during his lifetime, to a place above that of the state itself and its institutional source of purity and power, in this case the Party. And the process is rendered all the more impressive by the opposite tendency predominant throughout the world—the *de*sacralization of men, words, and virtually everything else. Rather than resort to the tone of uneasy contempt so frequent in Western observers, we do better to take a closer look at some of the psychological and historical currents involved.

All cultures have a way of rendering sacred the word ("In the beginning was the Word and the Word was with God, and the Word was God"); and none more than China. Relevant here is the Confucian focus upon the *name* as a means of ordering all human life. The traditional principle of "rectification of names" required not only that each live according to the rules governing his category of existence ("Let the ruler be ruler, the minister be minister; let the father be father and the son, son"), but that where disparity existed, the *man* undergo whatever moral change was required for him to fit the name. As the French sinologist Marcel Granet has written: "The name possesses the individual rather than the individual possess[ing] the name. It is inalienable." We may say that the "name"—for example, family name—was the immortal element toward which lay the major responsibility of the individual, himself a mere transient. Only through harmony with the name could a man achieve true "sincerity" or "the way of Heaven" —a place within the immortal rhythms that provided a Chinese equivalent to a state of grace.

The nature of Chinese characters, and traditional attitudes toward them, also enhance the power of the word. As ideographs, or what might be called formative images, they possess an evocative symbolic force beyond that of words in alphabetical scripts. Moreover, the traditional education and examination systems were so arranged that the memorization of specific groups of characters—those containing the society's ideal moral image of itself—was one's access to public life. This in turn meant entering what was for the Chinese a special realm of recorded history, so that one's relationship to words became a major path to symbolic immortality.

Within its own idiom Chinese Communism has perpetuated much of this kind of emphasis, and it is in such a cultural context that one must view Mao's own way with words. He has by no means been merely the bearer of venerable tendencies. Rather he has made use over the years of a word-centered tradition in the special fashion of a great contemporary leader.

Western students of Mao's thought have had some difficulty explaining the sources of its power. While often disagreeing on the question of whether Mao has demonstrated originality as a Marxist, most have rightly stressed his persistent preoccupation with themes of "struggle" and "contradictions" and "rectification" and "reform." But what has not been adequately reorganized, I believe, is a characteristic quality of tone and content that, more than any other, shaped the psychic contours of the Cultural Revolution. I refer to a kind of existential absolute, an insistence upon all-or-none confrontation with death. Mao always further insists that the confrontation be rendered meaningful, that it be associated with a mode of transcendence. One must risk all, not only because one has little to lose but because even in death one has much to gain.

This quality of thought is amply illustrated by many selections contained in the little red bible of the Cultural Revolution, *Quotations from Chairman Mao Tse-tung*.

One important chapter takes its title from Mao's 1944 essay "Serve the People," which was one of the most emphasized of all of his writings over the course of the entire movement. The chapter begins with a quotation advocating that all "serve the Chinese people heart and soul" and ends with two comments about death and dying taken from the 1944 essay. The first presents a simple definition of a **"worthy death"**:

> "Wherever there is struggle there is sacrifice, and death is a common occurrence. But we have the interests of the people and the sufferings of the great majority at heart, and when we die for the people it is a worthy death.
>
> "All men must die, but death can vary in its significance. The ancient Chinese writer Szuma Chien said, 'Though death befalls all men alike, it may be heavier than Mount Tai or lighter than a feather.' To die for the people is heavier than Mount Tai, but to work for the fascists and die for the exploiters and oppressors is lighter than a feather."

Here "weight" is equated with lasting significance: A death becomes "heavier than Mount Tai" because it contributes to the immortal revolutionary process of the Chinese people. Mao encourages everyone to cultivate such a death and thereby, during life, enhance his individual *sense* of immortality.

Another chapter, "War and Peace," contains passages (from essays originally written during the late thirties) that condemn unjust war but extol revolutionary war as "an antitoxin which not only eliminates the enemy's poison but also purges us of our own filth," and as "endowed with tremendous power [that] can transform many things or clear the way for their transformation." There is Mao's proud declaration: "Yes, we are advocates of the omnipotence of revolutionary war; that is good, not bad, it is Marxist." Here "omnipotence" refers on one level to policy priority, but on another to a sense of unlimited revolutionary power called forth by the purifying experience of facing death on behalf of a just cause.

Above all, one need not be afraid of death at the hands of the enemy—as suggested in a passage published originally in 1938:

"When we see the enemy, we must not be frightened to death like a rat who sees a cat, simply because he has a weapon in his hands. ... We are men, the enemy is also composed of men, we are all men so what should we fear? The fact that he has weapons? We can find the way to seize his weapons. All we are afraid of is getting killed by the enemy. But when we undergo the oppression of the enemy to such a point as this, how can anyone still fear death? And if we do not fear death, then what is there to fear about the enemy? So when we see the enemy, whether he is many or few, we must act as though he is bread that can satisfy our hunger, and immediately follow him."

Underneath the assumption that oppression is worse than death is a characteristically Maoist tone of transcendence, a message to the revolutionary that seems to say that death does not really exist for him; he has absolutely nothing to fear.

To eliminate awe of seemingly powerful enemies, Mao adopts an attitude of general leveling and de-immortalization. But this leveling is mere prelude to claiming that immortal status for his own revolutionary group, and declaring its consequent immunity to the emanations from ordinary arbiters of life and death, supernatural and historical. The revolutionary, then (as Mao also wrote in *Basic Tactics*), can wholeheartedly "resolve to fight to the death to kill the enemy."

A leader who can instill these transcendent principles in his followers can turn the most extreme threat and disintegration into an ordered certainty of mission, convert the most incapacitating death anxiety into a death-conquering calm of near-invincibility. He can in fact become the omnipotent guide sought by all totalist movements—precisely the meaning of the characterization of Mao during the Cultural Revolution as the "Great Leader, Great Teacher, Great Supreme Commander, the Great Helmsman." The thought of Mao becomes not so much an exact blueprint for the future as a "Way," a call to a particular mode of being on behalf of a transcendent purpose.

There are two psychological assumptions long prominent in Mao's thought but never so overtly insisted upon as during the Cultural Revolution. The first is an image of the human mind as infinitely malleable, capable of being reformed, transformed, and rectified without limit. The second is a related vision of the will as all-powerful, even to the extent that (in his own words) "The subjective creates the objective." That is, man's capacity for both undergoing change and changing his environment is unlimited; once he makes the decision for change, the entire universe can be bent to his will. But again the controlling image is the sense of revolutionary immortality that confers these vaulting capacities upon the mind. And the key to psychic malleability and power—the central purpose of the thought-reform process—is the replacement of prior modes of immortality (especially the biological one provided by the Chinese family system) with the newer revolutionary modes: those of the biosocial revolutionary "family" of enduring revolutionary "works," and of transcendent revolutionary enthusiasm.

A remarkable feature of the Cultural Revolution has

been its concretization of this entire process, so that Mao the man and the "thought of Mao Tse-tung" converge in an immortalizing corpus. Mao came to be regularly described in the Chinese press as "the greatest genius today," and all were assured that "Where the thought of Mao Tse-tung shines, there people see the way to fight for their liberation and there is hope for the victory of revolution." Also highly significant was the merging of this man-thought corpus with the larger immortal cultural-revolutionary substance we have spoken of, the merging of Mao with "the masses":

> "Chairman Mao . . . has the greatest trust in and the greatest concern for the masses, and the greatest support for their revolutionary movements and initiative."

The Maoist corpus then takes on the important function of serving as "a fundamental watershed" for distinguishing people from non-people:

> "Chairman Mao is the great standard bearer of the international Communist movement of the contemporary age, the most beloved and revered leader of the Chinese people and revolutionary peoples of the world. The thought of Mao Tse-tung is contemporary Marxism-Leninism of the highest level, a powerful ideological weapon against imperialism, revisionism, and dogmatism. To support or oppose Chairman Mao and the thought of Mao Tse-tung is a fundamental watershed dividing Marxism from revisionism, and revolution from counter-revolutionism."

The thought itself is sacralized—spoken of as "a compass and spiritual food" of which "every word . . . is as good as ten thousand words." The writings of Chairman Mao become

> "the best books in the world, the most scientific books, the most revolutionary books. . . . There have never

been writings even in China or abroad like the writings of Chairman Mao. . . . They develop Marxism, Leninism, they are The Peak in the modern world of Marxism-Leninism. There are peaks in the mountains but the highest peak is called The Peak."

And this sacred quality of Maoist thought is in turn directly associated with the desired revolutionary totalism:

"One has to be totally revolutionary. There are total and non-total revolutionaries. Some men are like that. You cannot say they are not revolutionaries; but they are not fully revolutionary. They are half revolutionary, half non-revolutionary. . . ."

The total revolutionary, as the same passage goes on to explain, is "ready to sacrifice his life" and is (to paraphrase Mao's own words) "not . . . afraid of wolves ahead and tigers behind . . . determined to change heaven and earth, fight the enemy, stick to the truth." Such dedication and courage are indeed possible insofar as one can genuinely worship Mao's thought along lines suggested by still another passage, which could well be viewed as the epitome of the immortalization of the word and all who embrace it:

"The thought of Mao Tse-tung is the sun in our heart, is the root of our life, is the source of all our strength. Through this, man becomes unselfish, daring, intelligent, able to do everything; he is not conquered by any difficulty and can conquer every enemy. The thought of Mao Tse-tung transforms man's ideology, transforms the fatherland . . . through this the oppressed people of the world will rise."

The Maoist corpus is elevated to an all-consuming prophecy: it nurtures men, predicts their future, and changes the world to accomplish its own prediction; it sets in motion spiritual forces against which nothing can stand.

This verbal genuflection before Mao has undoubtedly at

times taken on qualities of tired ritual—a cliché for all occasions. And the staggering claims often made in the Chinese press for the application of these thoughts contribute to the instant ridicule with which they have been so widely greeted. Yet here again the matter bears closer scrutiny. The most famous target of ridicule was the insistence, early in the Cultural Revolution, that the thoughts of Mao had been responsible for China's brilliant success in international table-tennis competition—and the mockery knew no bounds when the news came out later that the world champion himself had been strongly criticized for various shortcomings and eventually arrested. But M. Rufford Harrison, president of the United States Table Tennis Association, was considerably less derisive in his commentary:

"The writings and spirit of Mao invade every match the Chinese play. The national team, before beginning play, recite Mao quotations to give them courage, and in the middle of a tense game a Chinese crowd will often chant Mao's sayings to spur their heroes on. It has a terrific psychological effect, seeming to drive them to feats of endurance and other exceptional efforts."

If we assume that Harrison speaks not as a Maoist but merely as an accurate observer, we are obliged to conclude that embracing the immortal corpus can indeed inspire unusual effort and accomplishment.

We may suspect similar combinations of ritualistic cliché and authenticity in widely disseminated claims of the marvelous contributions of Mao's thought to such large tasks as the drilling of oil wells, the construction of great modern airports, and the completion in record time of highly advanced and elaborate equipment for the steel industry. And when we are told how villagers, in true Maoist fashion, have "transformed heaven and earth" in achieving enormous victories over wind, sand, flood, and drought, there is no reason for us to doubt that some of the people involved in these projects felt energized by the Maoist phrases being chanted—any more than we would doubt that many who did not said that they did. Concerning the claim that Mao's thought was responsible for the unexpectedly early completion and successful testing of a hydrogen bomb (in June 1967), we have reason to believe that the major contribution of Maoism was to leave the nuclear scientists alone. But who is to say that none of them—and none of the technicians and soldiers later praised for their courageous achievements in entering the test area to evaluate the bomb's effects—were sustained at all by the death-defying Maoist images we have discussed?

One might be tempted to dismiss the entire cult of Mao and his thought as no more than sycophantic indulgence of an old man's vanity were it not for the life Mao has lived and the impact he has made upon the Chinese people. He has in fact come close to living out precisely the kind of existential absolute he has advocated. No 20th-century life has come closer than his to the great myth of the hero— with its "road of trials," or prolonged death encounter, and its mastery of that encounter in a way that enhances the life of one's people.

His message of the mastery of death anxiety, reinforced by personal example, took on special relevance for a people living through a period (the first half of the 20th century) in which such anxiety was continuously mobilized by extreme dislocation, violence, and loss. During such times there is a hunger for words and acts that contribute to the re-ordering and "resymbolization" of collective existence.

At a more personal level we have noted Mao's preoccupation with his own series of survivals of intimate family members and revolutionary comrades. Mao's first wife and their son, his younger sister, and his two younger brothers all met violent deaths while serving the Chinese Communist movement. Mao lost his last sibling when his brother Mao Tse-min was executed in 1943 by a warlord (who had suddenly switched allegiance from the Communists to the Nationalists); and since Mao had actively guided and directed his brother's revolutionary career, this death must have engendered in him especially strong feelings of what I have elsewhere called guilt over survival priority. There is much evidence that Mao felt very strongly not only about these losses but about the manner in which they occurred. He has frequently revealed unusual sensitivity to death imagery in general and to survivor guilt in particular. But rather than being incapacitated by such feelings, he has, in the manner of all great leaders, applied them to the larger historical crises of his day.

One could draw upon a number of examples. For instance, in 1919, when Mao was still a little-known apprentice revolutionary editing a periodical in Changsha, a young girl of that city, whose parents had forced her to marry against her will, committed suicide. Mao was sufficiently moved by the incident to write nine newspaper articles in 13 days denouncing the old society's restrictions upon individual liberty and expecting a future "great wave of the freedom to love." Leaving aside the historical irony of his own later imposition of restrictions in many ways greater than those he condemned as a young libertarian, we note his unusually strong reaction to an individual death. Here and on other occasions he could embrace a form of death guilt that could be put to social use.

We may speak of this as an activist response to death— whether the death be of an immediate biological kind (as in this case) or of the more symbolic kind exemplified by chaos and injustice. The necessary combination for this response is full openness to death anxiety and death guilt, and an immediate transcendence of these emotions through linking them directly to revolutionary struggles. And without attempting to detail Mao's remarkable achievements, we may say that this combination has greatly contributed to his revitalizing talents as a peasant organizer, military strategist, Party leader, head of state, and general theorist in the "Sinification" of Marxism.

Mao's relationship to the myth of the hero is also strengthened by certain qualities of personal and revolutionary style that reveal a man closely attuned to the pulse of immortality. One such trait is his celebrated "revolutionary romanticism," a designation that would sound highly derogatory to most Communist ears but that official Chinese commentaries have associated with courage in the face of objective difficulties, and with great revolutionary vision (to be distinguished, of course, from *non*revolutionary romanticism, regarded as an unrealistic expression of philosophical idealism). The image of the revolutionary romanticist has been fostered by Mao's series of brilliantly conducted guerrilla campaigns during the twenties and thirties and by his writings about these campaigns; by his continuing combination of "guerrilla ethos" and "heaven-storming" approach to the transformation of Chinese society, combining heroic effort with extreme austerity (on the order of the old slogan of millet plus rifles"); and by his general affinity for outlaws, and for the romantic aura often bestowed by Chinese tradition upon outlaws as noble subverters of prevailing social evil. For such reasons a Chinese writer once called Mao "fundamentally a character from a Chinese novel or opera." And Stuart Schram speaks of his "military romanticism," by which he means Mao's tendency to "regard war as the supreme adventure and the supreme test of human courage and human will," along with a "warlike quality of his temperament and imagination [that leads him to] pose economic and even scientific and philosophical problems in these terms." Mao's revolutionary romanticism, then, is the hero's quest for doing more than the possible, risking and even courting death in order to alter the meaning of both death and life, "storming heaven" and challenging the claims of existing deities, political as well as theological, in order to replace them with the claims of revolutionary immortality. Associated with this romantic affinity for transcendence have been some of Mao's greatest achievements (the Communist victory itself and the revitalization of China) as well as his most spectacular failures (the Great Leap Forward and perhaps the Cultural Revolution).

It becomes clear that from the time of his youth Mao has felt himself deeply involved in a struggle to restore national pride—which over the years became nothing less than a heroic quest to reassert the life power of China. Hence, Mao came to associate Communism with the timeless virtues of the peasant masses and of the Chinese earth. And his relentless pursuit of the thought-reform process has been an effort to cement this association, especially within the minds of intellectuals. Mao once described his Communist movement as "passionately concerned with the fate of the Chinese nation, and moreover with its fate throughout all eternity." And one recalls Mao's ringing declaration, upon his victorious assumption of power in 1949, that China had "stood up" and would "never again be an insulted nation"—an expression of national resurgence that was as authentically Maoist as it was Chinese. Rather than speak of Mao as a "father figure" or "mother figure" for his countrymen (no doubt he has been both), we do better to see him as a death-conquering hero who became the embodiment of Chinese immortality.

It has often been said that a historical innovator manages to interpret the most fundamental experiences of his generation. Such experiences inevitably involve coping with death and achieving symbolic immortality; we may say that Mao has done precisely that, always with an impulse toward the transcendent, and not only for his own generation. His accomplishments and inclinations rendered him a likely candidate for the excesses of virtue with which the Cultural Revolution was to anoint him.

Over the course of Mao's later career the word becomes not only flesh but *his* flesh. The man-word corpus is increasingly represented as *absolutely* identical with China's destiny. And we sense that we are witnessing the tragic transition from the great leader to the despot.

Mao's active participation in the creation of his own cult has become increasingly clear. His rewriting of earlier works is consistent with practices of other modern Communist leaders, and also with those of premodern Chinese emperors in the process of enthroning themselves and establishing new dynasties. But Mao seems to go further than anyone else in the infusion of his man-word corpus into every psychological cranny of Chinese existence.

Mao apparently requires the immortalizing corpus for his "romantic" sense of self and history, his image of heroic confrontation with the powers of heaven and earth. The extremities of the deification would seem to confirm his highly active complicity in the process, and his loss of perspective concerning its wider impact. One thinks of the shock and disgust of Eastern European audiences when reviewing dramatic performances by visiting Chinese troupes in which the image of Mao became almost literally a diety.

A great leader turns into a despot when he loses confidence in his claim to immortality. Then, feeling himself threatened by biological and symbolic death, he becomes obsessed with survival as such. He is no longer able to put his death guilt effectively in the service of a noble mission, and instead becomes an "eternal survivor" who requires the defeat or death of a never-ending series of "enemies" in order to reactivate his own life and revive his ever-faltering sense of immortality. We may then suspect that he depends heavily upon the mechanism of denial—upon the fantasy "I am *not* losing my power, I am *not* dying." He resorts to ever more desperate and magical efforts at achieving vitality. Since no one can provide the power over death that is sought, all become enemies, and we begin to observe something close to the Caligula-like state I have described elsewhere as "survivor paranoia." (I am not suggesting that Mao is mad, nor am I making a clinical psychiatric diagnosis of any kind; there is no convincing evidence for such a diagnosis. Moreover, one must be very cautious about applying individual psychopathological terms to collective behavior. What I am suggesting by the phrase "survivor paranoia" as possibly relevant to Mao is a state of mind affecting aging leaders, after long and repeated survivor-like crises, in which there can be certain paranoid contours.)

Also involved is an old man's fear that he is losing his "potency." In speaking of the potency of a great revolutionary, I refer by no means only to his sexual capacity or physical strength, but to the special power of one who has felt himself to be a transmitter of forces shaping the destiny of mankind. Here it is instructive to compare Mao with Gandhi. We may say that in old age both experienced this sense of declining power, and that both sought to revitalize themselves through reassertion of purity. In Gandhi's case that purity took the form of a personal demonstration of control: his sleeping with naked young girls as a form of experiment with temptation and exercise in sexual restraint. Both men sought to buttress a relationship to the eternal by calling upon the purity and life power of the young.

But where Gandhi looked upon this aspect of his struggle as a private discipline, Mao enlarged his quest for purity to include the whole of China and staked the future of an entire revolution upon it. This is not to suggest that the Cultural Revolution is a product merely of Mao's intrapsychic struggles; but rather that such inner struggles now spread confusion and antagonism, rather than the illumination they had in the past. The bold stroke of a leader, threatened by loss of personal and revolutionary power, becomes the despotic turbulence of an eternal survivor.

In classical psychoanalytic terms one could view the entire process as "the death of the father"—the aging leader's reluctance to permit the inevitable ascendancy of his assertive "sons." But it may be more accurate to speak of it as "the death of the word." The capacity of the revolutionary-Maoist combination of words and images to mediate between inner and outer worlds is, at least temporarily, moribund. Hence Mao's plunge into psychism, into a one-sided focus upon intrapsychic purity at the expense of extrapsychic reality. In place of his formerly sensitive application of personal passions to China's desperate historical experience, we encounter instead a substitution of his own history for history at large. Because he and a few around him fear the death of the Revolution, China must be made to convulse. The leader turns inward toward an increasingly idiosyncratic and extreme vision of immortality, and demands that his vision be permanently imprinted upon all. Mao's actions belie his stated willingness to leave assessments of present revolutionary developments to future generations. As much as any leader in recent centuries he seeks to chart and control history and "fix its course for centuries to come." The more resistance to this course he encounters among the living, the more he looks toward the future and seeks vindication from the unborn.

The Chinese Cultural Revolution, then, is the last stand of a great revolutionary against internal and external forces pressing him along that treacherous path from hero to despot. It is similarly the last stand of a collective expression of early revolutionary glory that he has epitomized. And it is perceived on several symbolic levels as a last stand against death itself—of the leader, the revolution, and individual man in general.

It is in the nature of great men and great revolutions to be dissatisfied with their accomplishments, however extraordinary, and to plunge into realms even they cannot conquer. If this be the meaning of tragedy, the tragedy is not merely theirs. Nor is the present task of recovering from Mao's excesses—and evolving an equilibrium between life and death appropriate to our age—that of China alone.
September 1968

The Red Guard

ALVIN W. GOULDNER/IRVING LOUIS HOROWITZ

"Judging from this evening you seem to be in good condition,"
I said. Mao Tse-tung smiled wryly and replied that there was
perhaps some doubt about that. He said again that he was getting
ready to see God very soon.

Interview with Mao Tse-tung, by Edgar Snow,
New Republic, Feb. 27, 1965.

In isolating ourselves from China, we have placed the
West in a situation where every turn in the Chinese Revolution seems inexplicably mysterious and in which we are
finally driven to explain mystery as due to madness. If the
Russian Revolution seemed to be a "mystery wrapped in an
enigma," the Chinese Revolution seems increasingly—to
certain Westerners—a mystery that enwraps and conceals a
core of madness. When political fears are compounded by
a confrontation with an alien culture the differences that
become visible seem to be an expression of insanity. The
explanation of political events as due to madness is a con-

fession of intellectual impotence; it is another way of saying that we are incapable of offering rational explanations for events.

Nothing seems more insane, at first blush, than the recent reports of street skirmishing of the Red Guards with workers and detachments of the Red Army sent to curb them, attacks of Red Guards upon the home of Madame Sun Yat-sen, their damage to certain public properties, and above all their clashes with select local Communist Party cadres and headquarters.

Our job here is to seek and propose a sociological framework in which even the seeming madness of the Red Guard episode may be made intelligible.

First, we ought to be clear about what it is that needs explaining. What is it that seems so mysterious to us in the West about the behavior of the Red Guards?

Surely we would not find it strange if it were some kind of *coup d'état* that had been perpetrated by a section of the army against the Communist Party or against the regime. We have seen that before in Latin America and in Indonesia. But despite its military designation, the Red Guard is not a wing of the army but basically is comprised of militant students, rural and urban youth—in some reports numbering as many as six million—who have remained more loyal to the ideals of the Revolution than to the organizational forms of the conventional Communist Party establishment. The Red Guard has put itself forward not as an opponent of Mao Tse-tung but, to the contrary, as his most vocal protector and truest follower. The avowed aim of the Red Guard is to protect Mao and his teachings and, indeed, to protect the entire Central Committee of the Communist Party. The Red Guards are a generation-cohort whose revolutionary fervor has not been blunted by *Realpolitik*.

What is strange, then, is that successful and established revolutionaries should incite and accept protection from student militants, even though the party hierarchy has created an enormous and far-ranging network of powerful institutions: the Communist Party, the Red army, a newly emerging bureaucracy in almost all sectors of life, and upon whom—one might think—they might confidently rely for the perpetuation of the revolution and its regime.

The central question, then, is why has Mao turned to the students and allowed them—and quite probably, incited them—to speak on his behalf, on behalf of the Central Committee of the Chinese Communist Party? And why has he done so in this particular period in the history of the Chinese Revolution?

The question of its timing, does not seem too difficult. Here, three considerations seem foremost. First, the succession problem grows increasingly critical with each passing year, and it must be seen as such by the old leaders of the Chinese Communist Party, who are already venerable even by Chinese standards. Unlike Western leaders such as Joseph Stalin and Charles de Gaulle whose public statements never intimated their mortality, Mao has for some time been publicly pondering his impending death. As his interviews with Edgar Snow and others indicate, he expects to die shortly. Whatever the publicity value of his recent swimming of the Yangtze river, it is clear that his private ratiocinations are somber; he is thoroughly aware of his own mortality and of its political implications.

Second, this intensifying succession crisis has developed in an international context in which the old leaders of the Chinese Communist Party have become increasingly aware of the possibility that their own revolution, like any other, might be corrupted if not overthrown. The Chinese struggle against the Soviet Union (and in particular what they conceive to be its "revisionism") has heightened their anxiety about the safety and future of the Chinese Revolution to which they have devoted their youth and their lives.

Third, the mobilization of the Red Guard can be considered as part of a general intensification of fervor as the international crisis deepens from the Chinese perspective. The Chinese have suffered diplomatic as well as political losses in such far-flung places as Cuba, where the Chinese regime was denounced by Castro; in Indonesia, where Sukarno has been replaced by Suharto as the actual leader of the regime and where the Chinese no less than the Communist Party have suffered intensive persecutions; in Africa, where Boumedienne's regime in Algeria replaced Ben Bella's thus causing the collapse of a major "third world" conference; and also, in Ghana where Nkrumah was displaced as leader precisely when he was on a state visit to China. All of these genuine setbacks have occasioned intensification of the internal conflicts. In some part the phenomenon of the Red Guards is an answer to these recent defeats: they announce that the Revolution still lives. The Red Guards provide the form, if not always the substance, of the permanent revolution.

In this connection, it should be kept in mind that within the framework of Marxism there has always been a strong wing deeply troubled by national revolutions at the expense of the continuation of the revolution elsewhere. Whatever the basic differences between Maoism and Trotskyism on this point, there seems a common fear that stability can only bring about the conservatizing of the revolution. The Red Guards in such a context can symbolize the viability of the revolution, if not provide a guarantee against its natural aging and decadence.

But where do Mao and his associates see the danger coming from? Here, it would be misleading if we sought to understand the Chinese Revolution on the model of the Russian. There is a continual temptation to misread Chinese history by seeing it as repeating the problems and the stages of the Russian Revolution. But this is misleading because the Chinese Revolution took place after, and developed in the context of, a prior and successful Soviet Revolution; the two can no more be expected to be the same than the second child in a family can be expected to be like the first.

One difference between the two revolutions is this: unlike the Chinese, the leaders of the Russian Revolution conceived of the danger to their revolution as coming, primarily and most powerfully, from the world outside. And with good reason. Immediately following upon the October Revolution the Bolsheviks found themselves beset by the armies of more than a dozen nations. The political trials of the old Bolsheviks and of others commonly sought to link their "betrayal" to the direct and deliberate intervention and scheming of foreign powers. Thus, even where the enemy was seen as being within, he was essentially defined as an "agent of a foreign power." The Stalinist conception of the danger and of the enemy was thus very largely centered on the outside world.

But this does not seem to be the case for the Chinese Revolution. Certainly, the Chinese Communists believe that Chaing Kai-shek would like to invade their mainland and that, to do so successfully, he must and might receive the support of the United States. They are similarly aware of the possibilities of being militarily embroiled with the United States in any extension of the war in Vietnam. Yet these "objective" dangers from without do not seem to be the dangers that weigh most heavily upon the minds of the aging Chinese Communist Party leaders, but, rather, the dangers that abide within their own culture.

The most essential point being made is not so much with respect to the location of the perceived dangers to the Revolution but, rather, with respect to the location of the perceived resources of and possible help to the Revolution. The Russian Bolsheviks, prior to the October Revolution, never believed in their own ability to bring the Russian Revolution to a successful culmination without international support. They expected that their seizure of power in Russia would be the signal for a European-wide, and especially a German, revolution from which they could receive aid for their own industrialization. They did not at first imagine they could overcome what they regarded as "Russian backwardness" without outside assistance from industrially advanced nations. When the German and Hungarian revolutions failed, after the Bolshevik seizure of power in Russia, the Russian revolutionaries were despairing and disoriented.

The Russian Revolution was, from its earliest inception, a special sort of social movement: a movement for cultural revitalization which saw the solution to its problems as deriving from the *importation* of Western technologies. Its attention was from the first fastened upon its relation to and its dependence upon the West. After the failure of the revolution in the West, the Soviet leaders remained sensitive to the manner in which their security and their prospects were contingent upon the new society's relationship to the outside world. Even when their anxiety and pessimism were overcome and bound by the slogan of "Socialism in One Country," the Soviet leaders never doubted that developments elsewhere—such as Fascism and Nazism—could (and were intended to) impair their new society. Russian intellectuals had long measured themselves by Western European standards and models and they continued to do so even when thrown back upon their own resources during the Stalinist "anti-cosmopolitan" period.

The Chinese revolutionists have, to the contrary, long despised their subjection to outside influences of Western imperialism and to what they took to be its *alien* culture. Their basic impulse was not to import Western cultural models, nor to emulate and overtake the West. Their basic impulse was to liberate themselves from such outside influences. In short, China was a colonially dominated nation in a way that Russia had not been.

The Chinese did not expect help from their former foreign colonial overlords. During the process of their gathering revolutionary efforts, from 1927 onward, they also found that the needs of their own revolution were being subordinated to those of the Russians. They began to view the Soviet Union not as a paragon of international revolutionary solidarity but rather as a more sophisticated expression of the nationalist selfishness of Western nations. They began to see the Soviet Union not as an example of revolutionary vitality but as a sad case of revolutionary corruption and softness demonstrated by the collapse of fervor among its own younger generation, the bureaucratization of Communist Party workers, and the rise of party careerism. These sentiments finally expressed themselves in the Chinese attack on Khrushchev's "revisionism," which was only one side of the coin. The other side entailed a demand that the revolution hew to its original purpose. They began to believe that the authenticity of the revolution depended more upon their internal spiritual purity than external material aid.

This internal preoccupation is evident in Mao's recurrent comments about the growing laxity of the Chinese youth, and of the possibility that they would not have the stomach to perpetuate the Chinese Revolution once he and his cohorts were gone. Again, it is just this sensitivity to the internal dangers that face the Chinese Revolution, and the willingness of the Chinese leaders to talk about them publicly—

as they did, for example, on their recent visits to Eastern Europe—that makes their political diagnoses of their own situation *seem* to be surprisingly realistic, and quite different in character from those typically enunciated by the Russian leaders.

But there is not only a question of how they define and conceive the *location* of these dangers to the Chinese Revolution. There is also the further and equally important problem of how they conceive of the *character* of these dangers. To understand this properly, to see what the Chinese regard as the source of their present danger, it is also necessary to see what they regard as the source of their previous *success* and victory. Here the matter must be set in its historical context and viewed as part of the long-range evolution of Communist strategy, from Marx onward.

A central shift in political strategy has occurred in the Communist world since the time of Marx. It has been a shift from a view which at first emphasized the importance of objective economic conditions for a successful revolution, to a view that increasingly emphasized the importance of political initiative, party organization, and ideological commitment. This shift was first fully visible in Lenin's objections to Plekhanov's doctrine of "spontaneity," which saw the revolution as a natural outgrowth of a mature working class. To this Lenin counterposed the need for a revolutionary elite that could seize and maintain the political initiative. The Chinese operated in an economy that was even less like that in which Marx had expected a socialist revolution than did the Russian Bolsheviks, and they developed an increasing emphasis upon the importance of ideology and the "spiritual factor" as the mainspring and ultimate guarantor of the revolution. The Chinese emphasis on dialectics, on the power of self-criticism, can be interpreted as a further move away from the original focus on economics which Marx held in common with the classical economists. If Lenin added to the Marxist corpus the concept of party organization as fundamental to revolution-making, Mao added to Leninism the concept of personal will and military fortitude as the essence of nation-building. In Maoism, Marxism has thus turned full-circle toward an unembarrassed "utopianism." It is the willful struggle—not the organizational machinery—that the aging leadership trusts. Thus the Chinese leadership is even ready to risk the possibility of internal strife, not because it is oblivious to the possibilities of ramifying civil conflict, but rather because it is more concerned with the purifying value of conflict.

The older generation of Chinese Communists had, certainly from an orthodox Marxist viewpoint, achieved something of a miracle ever since their long march north to the Shensi province in 1927. By classical Marxist standards they could very well feel that they had achieved the impossible. For they had come to power in a country which was even more industrially backward and economically depressed than revolutionary Russia, and in which modern science, modern industry, and modern technology scarcely existed.

Indeed, it was only when the Chinese Communists abandoned orthodox Bolshevik tactics that victories were registered. In the early 1920's, they tried to capture large cities, such as Canton, where it was hoped the factory workers would rally to the revolutionary cause; but such strata were either too small or too intimidated to forge a revolutionary phalanx. But when the Communists were driven from the cities to the countryside, they changed not only their tactical emphasis from factory workers to peasants, but more significantly, their leadership—from the Moscow-trained cadres who had secret headquarters in Shanghai to indigenous Chinese elements (Chu Teh was a war lord, and Mao himself was of peasant origins) operating in the open. Thus, the victories of the Chinese Communists coincided with a turn from town to countryside, from Bolshevik to native party cadres, and from clandestine to military actions.

The "miracle" of the Chinese Revolution was thus even greater than that of the Russian Revolution, not simply because of the industrial backwardness of Chiang's China in comparison to Czarist Russia, but because the Chinese Revolution succeeded in totally reorienting the temperament of the rural masses no less than the urban classes, whereas the Russian Revolution only reoriented a strata of the working classes. The Chinese Red Army smashed the Kuomintang in civil war. This experience also reemphasized the role of "will" in the making of the Chinese Revolution in contrast to the role of organization.

In short, their political and military experience leads the old Chinese leaders to conceive of themselves as having succeeded, not because of "objective factors," but rather because of "subjective factors"—because of correct theory, because of a steadfast commitment to ideology, because of a readiness for personal sacrifice. It is precisely this that leads them to emphasize the importance of the teachings of Mao Tse-tung. This emphasis on Mao's writings is not, as is sometimes suggested, to be understood simply as a part of the process of the deification of Mao. It is rather their conception of the meaning of Chinese experience: namely, that it was theory, indeed Mao's theory, that had made the primary difference for them and not objective conditions. In the hands of Mao, Marxism more than ever became a doctrine to live by rather than a dogma to abide by, and it is at this level that their exhortation to read and study Mao seems most intelligible.

In addition there has been a long-standing, if concealed, chasm between the struggling Communist movement of China and the established Bolshevik organization of the Soviet Union. From the 1920's onward it was clear that Stalin was less concerned with fostering the Chinese revolution than with maintaining a legal correctness in his dealings with foreign nations that could provide a protective international framework for the Soviet Union. The Chinese were not merely disappointed with the withdrawal of Soviet aid once their own revolution succeeded, but were newly convinced of the parochial national character and bureaucratization of the Soviet revolution. The conversion of Chinese Marxism into a mass movement, such as that exhibited by the Red Guards, is an attempt to compensate for the loss of material foreign aid by strengthening their internal spiritual resources. For this reason the Chinese have ordered many slogans concerning the power of ideas to be put forward as a last gasp against the frustrations and inhibitions occasioned by the inexorable technological advance of Bolshevik Russia, no less than capitalist United States. Indeed, it might be said that Chinese Marxism-Maoism is the ultimate romanticization of Socialist doctrine; it is the elevation to a supreme level of the role of heart over that of head, of will over economic conditions, and people over weaponry.

The old Chinese leadership understand their past success as the product of their will and ideological commitment. At the same time, this is how they understand their failure, or at least the threat of possible failure that they see hanging over them with the passing of the older generation. Because their political experience has led the Chinese to assign so much significance to the importance of theoretical, ideological, and spiritual factors, they have come to define their present danger—no less than their former victory—as deriving from a decline in ideological commitment and from a loss of theoretical clarity. Correspondingly, if the danger is ideological and spiritual, then they must also see the solution and remedy as being ideological and spiritual. And that seems to be why the current turbulence in China has come to center upon the problem of the completion of what is conceived to be a "cultural" revolution, and thus on the need to complete the transformation of the values and beliefs of the Chinese people.

The aging Chinese political elite is a charismatic cohort: it not only stands above the institutions which it has created, but it also does not fully trust them—and indeed more than mildly distrusts them. It distrusts them, in some part, because it recognizes that some sectors and echelons in these new institutions, many composed of men immediately beneath them, have been trained in Moscow. They are thus not simply politically suspect on nationalistic grounds but also may be seen as ideologically contaminated by Russian revisionism. And in one way this is quite realistic. Some Russian intellectuals have not entirely despaired of reconciliation with the Chinese because when the old leaders die they will be replaced by young men who have been students of the Russians. But the aging Chinese leaders not only distrust these younger leaders; they also and more generally distrust all the institutions that they man, for they believe that the life of the revolution is in the *spirit* and not in its institutions.

What then are the Central Committee and the Chinese leadership attempting to do in unleashing the Red Guards? Fundamentally, they are seeking a revival of spirit and the purification of revolutionary ideology. The older generation is seeking to bypass part of the Moscow-tainted middle generation, and provide a check upon it, by allying itself with an ideologically reinvigorated younger generation. They are seeking to foster revolutionary fervor among a generation that has never known revolution, and thereby to commit this generation to a posture of ideological purity, thus providing a stable framework that will insure the continuity of the revolution, as they conceive it.

In unleashing the Red Guards the Chinese Central Committee has also unlocked certain doors to social change. There were, indeed, middle class styles and Western importations in Chinese urban regions. There were indeed 5 percent men who lived off their previous commercial and land holdings. There were, indeed, bureaucrats unable or unwilling to perform everyday services in a competent manner. It would be a mistake to think that the enemy of the Red Guards is entirely a fiction. The enemy within was real, so much so that the Chinese leaders were willing to risk a paralysis of industrialization to combat it. It could well be that the Red Guards form the fighting wing of a twentieth century Chinese puritanism, for their demand for purification has been made in the name of simplification of life styles, improving of work styles, and ordering of cultural styles. The fervor, the passion of such a movement may easily spill over into violence of an unbridled variety, but of a kind not unknown in the West and frequently found among those who are most fervently concerned with the purification of the spirit. The risks of the present course of action on the part of the Chinese leadership are indeed great. Undoubtedly they believe the possible consequences of its failure will be greater still.

One possible consequence of promoting the Red Guards may be to break the legitimation system of orthodox Communists. Instead of a system that operates through the organizational channels of the Communist Party system, the

Red Guards symbolize a return to spontaneity and to the importance of ideological purity rather than party loyalty. The wheels for such an approach were already set in motion by the emphasis on "national liberation" movements outside the orthodox Communist Party apparatus in many parts of the "third world." Khrushchev, in his critique of Maoism made just prior to his retirement, exhibited considerable fears lest such emphasis on liberation movements turn into "anti-party" vehicles. It might well be that the Chinese leadership has taken the next logical step, and declared that the protection of the Chinese Revolution is no longer to be the exclusive duty of the "vanguard party," but rather of the people as a whole. In short, neither charismatic nor bureaucratic routinization now obtains. Rather, China is witnessing a restructuring of both—made in a holy alliance between the militant antiquarians who have nothing to lose but their waning leadership and the militant youths who have nothing to lose but their reason for living.

If bypassing the middle generation—the transitional generation—can spare China the agonies of Stalinist totalitarianism, then the results of the "cultural revolution" may well come to be judged as positive—even in the West. However, if this new generational coalition should tear Chinese culture apart in the name of ideological purity, it might well be that instead of sparing China the worst disruptions of the Soviet experience, it will make that seem a model of orderly evolution.

November 1966